And now, *How to Get Your Husband to Talk to You:*

"Don't miss this book! It's fun, realistic, smart, helpful—on every page. Mind you, I don't have any feelings about it. We're talking straight problem-solving here... Think of it as an armchair travel book, an interplanetary cruise, a Grunt-English dictionary. Think of it as 'your husband is a TV,' and you—for once—have the remote."

—DAVID KOPP, COAUTHOR, WITH HEATHER HARPHAM-KOPP
Love Stories God Told AND *Praying the Bible for Your Marriage*

"*How to Get Your Husband to Talk to You* addresses an age-old question asked by all women in love. Connie and Nancy offer a fresh reminder to honor and accept your man. You'll learn how to frame your words, diminish your details, and acknowledge your differences. The authors' warm, story-vignette style of writing makes this book an easy, quick read."

—DONNA OTTO, SPEAKER AND AUTHOR OF
The Gentle Art of Mentoring
FOUNDER OF HOMEMAKERS BY CHOICE

Nancy Cobb
Connie Grigsby

HOW to get your HUSBAND to TALK to YOU

Multnomah® Publishers *Sisters, Oregon*

HOW TO GET YOUR HUSBAND TO TALK TO YOU
published by Multnomah Publishers, Inc.

International Standard Book Number: 978-1-590-52727-6

Printed in the United States of America

For information:
MULTNOMAH PUBLISHERS, INC. • 601 N. LARCH ST. • SISTERS, OR 97759

LIBRARY OF CONGRESS CATALOGING-IN-PUBLICATION DATA
Cobb, Nancy, 1938–
How to get your husband to talk to you / by Nancy Cobb & Connie Grigsby. p.cm.
ISBN 1-57673-771-3 1. Interpersonal communication. 2. Man-woman relationships.
3. Men—Psychology. I. Grigsby, Connie. II. Title
BF637.C45C622001 302.2—dc21 2001000543

06 07 08 09 10 11 10 9 8 7 6
146673257

To my beloved Ray.
Thank you for your love and encouragement.
There's no one I'd rather listen to than you.
I treasure our life together.
To our precious children: Stuart and Kathy; Paul;
Chrissy and Rod; Anne; and grandson Justin.
Your love and support continue to spur me on.
To my darling sister, Christine.
Your Christlike example continues to impact my life,
as does your love.
To Connie.
What a gift your friendship is to me.
I thank God for you.

NANCY COBB

To my three sisters:
Debbie, Beverly, and Anita.
What a joy it was growing up with you....
You were my first girlfriends, and
what wonderful memories we share:
Bethel, bicycles, bat and ball,
flip-flops, hand-me-downs, lightning bugs,
cornstarch pudding, pop, Elgin owls,
neighbors, family, one another.
I love you and your families very much.
To Nancy,
my trusted friend and mentor.
When I think of spiritual giants, I will always think of you.
To my many friends with whom I am so richly blessed.
From Teresa in first grade right up 'til today.
You are precious to me.

CONNIE GRIGSBY

contents

part one: About Him
Why Can't He Be More Like Me?

part two: More about Him
Different Strokes for Different Folks

part three: about you

I Didn't Know That!

part four: About the Two of You

Lighting the Coals of Communication

part five: About the Relationship

Keeping the Fire Going

Foreword

Nancy and Connie have filled this book with wise and wonderful counsel on understanding the differences between how men and women communicate. *How to Get Your Husband to Talk to You* is a treasure of personal experiences, tried and true ideas, and seasoned insights on marriage. My husband and I have been married 44 years, and how I wish I'd had this book in the early years!

Whether you're a new bride or have been married for a long time, following the advice in this book can greatly improve your marriage. What a positive difference it makes when you learn how to relate to your husband in a way he understands! My husband felt frustrated and lost the point when I tried to give him the "book-length version" of whatever I needed to tell him. Our communication improved greatly once I discovered that my husband was better able to hear the "condensed" version. So I learned to vent my feelings and share in detail with women friends—while giving my husband the necessary facts—as this book will show you.

Following the wise counsel here can help you make your marriage better than ever. You may even fall in love with your husband all over again!

SHEILA CRAGG
CREATOR OF WWW.WOMANSWALK.COM

Acknowledgments

To Nancy Thompson, our dear, wonderful friend and trusted editor. Your excellence in what you do and your commitment in seeing this project through inspired us time and again. You'll never know how encouraging those e-mail notes were (Hang in there! We're almost done! You can do it!). We'll always treasure the time we had together in Omaha, and look forward to many more gatherings in the future. Once again, it was a joy to work with you.

To our husbands, children, and extended family. Your support, cheers, hugs, and unconditional love put the wind in our sails time and again. Thank you for praying and caring. We love you.

To our many friends who prayed us through this project. What a blessing it was to know that you were praying on our behalf. Thank you, special friends.

To the Noble Men class at Christ Community Church. Thank you for your openness in sharing your thoughts and insights.

To Multnomah Publishers. Thanks for giving two authors the thrill of writing their second book! We count it a privilege to be part of your family.

And most of all, thanks be to God, who saw us through every step of the way. We give all the glory and praise to Him.

INTRODUCTION

We know why you picked up this book! You want your relationship with your husband to wake up conversationally. You want to talk to your husband, and you want him to talk to you.

Think for a moment about traveling to a foreign island. If you want to communicate with the natives once you get there, you have two choices: You can either learn to speak their language, or you can hire a translator. Smiling, laughing, and pointing will help you communicate to a degree, but if you want to establish a rich, meaningful relationship with the people, you must learn their native tongue.

The same is true in marriage. When you married your husband, not only did you choose to visit a foreign country, in a sense, but you chose to live there as well—until death do you part! You probably thought, as we did, that at least one native on the island spoke your language—your husband. But you quickly discovered you were wrong! Not only did he not speak it; he didn't seem to have a clue regarding the basics of your language—feelings, nurturing, and cherishing, to name a few. Not to mention the "everyday talk" of toilet paper rolls, remote controls, driving habits, taking out the trash, and setting wet objects on wooden furniture.

The deal is, men don't speak women! And because they don't, you have the same two choices that the traveler had: Hire a translator (this doesn't seem very appealing to us), or learn to speak your husband's language. *How to Get Your Husband to Talk to You* is about the latter. It will help you become fluent in your husband's language so that you can begin to communicate with him in a fresh, revitalized way.

We surveyed hundreds of men, and 80 percent of them said they want to talk to their wives (we're guessing the other 20 percent were thinking about the previous night's football game!). We solicited feedback from these men as to why they are clamming up. Their observations and the suggestions we include will help you overcome the silence in your marriage.

You will begin to see why men do the things they do, and why they love to solve your problems. You'll start to see things through the grid of their lives, and you will learn some surprising things about yourself as well: Hormones! Sex! Places you don't want to go! There is a chapter on developing thicker skin, which addresses the number one reason men say they don't talk more—their wives overreact to what is being said!

Perhaps you've backed your husband into a corner because he feels he can never say the right thing or that he says it incorrectly. This book will help you stop doing that. It may also cause your husband to see you in a new light as you begin to put some of these principles to work. He will be thrilled to discover that he is free to be himself once again.

What a relief this is to a man. What a relief, too, to be married to a woman who speaks his native tongue.

This book is not about manipulation. And it isn't about "getting" your husband to do anything. It is really about you. You can't change another's behavior, but you can change your own. It's interesting what happens when you do this, for often your changed behavior will elicit change in another that nothing else could. But again, that's not what this book is about. It is about what you can do and say and think and change that will create an inviting climate for warm conversation. You will discover that as you do this, a peace will enter your heart that wasn't there before, regardless of whether your husband responds.

As you read, keep in mind that we speak from a general frame of reference. Each person is different and unique, and not every statement will apply to every person.

Also, just glancing through the table of contents will give you an idea of the many topics that we will talk about. Don't feel overwhelmed or think there's too much to learn. *How to Get Your Husband to Talk to You* is fun and practical—an easy-to-read primer of sorts that will help you resolve the age-old mystery of communication between the sexes. You can open this book to any section and pick up a tip or two that will encourage your husband to talk to you. So whether you have lots of time to read or just a few minutes a week, we think you'll find this book helpful.

Are you ready for change? Are you ready to speak your husband's native tongue? Are you ready for your husband to talk to you?

We hope that you are, and we suspect he's ready, too! There is one thing you can count on: God will give you all the help you need.

part one

About Him

why can't he be more like me?

What is a husband?
He's the one who, with a touch,
can bring back the starlight and glow
of years long ago. . . .
At least he thinks he can—
don't disappoint him.

ALAN BECK

A woman waxes poetic when she meets the man of her dreams. She exclaims, *"He is so different from anyone I have ever met."*

She begins mentally listing the attributes of his character and physique, his personality, his likes and dislikes. They talk for hours about their hopes and dreams for the future. She concludes that she can't live without him. She thinks about him all the time and lives for the times when they are together. She could talk forever about him and does.

As their wedding day approaches, stardust still filling her eyes, she says that he acts as though she is the only person on earth. She loves it that he speaks his mind and finds it charming that he occasionally nods off in the movies, making a sweet sound like a humming bee.

But something seems to happen almost the minute the bride takes off her veil. It isn't long before she is spending a lot of time reexamining her precious new groom. That charming bee sound is now slightly annoying, as is his tendency to say what he thinks about her formerly undiscussed foibles.

Does he not notice that there are whiskers in the sink when he finishes shaving? Does he think that toilet paper rolls just automatically reattach themselves to the dispenser? How does he think the dishes actually get into the cabinet?

She begins to think (and possibly to share with others), he is so different from anyone I have ever met. But her implication is not the same as it was in the beginning.

You are in for a delightful trip down a path you may not have explored in a very long time. This first section will lift the curtain on some of the differences between men and women. Your husband should love being a man, and you should love it that he is one. It will be such a relief to both of you when you accept him as he is. He is worth it!

chapter one

MEN EXPRESS LOVE BY DOING

One of the fundamental differences between men and women is the way they express love. Men are goal-oriented and express love by *doing*, while women are relationship-oriented and express love by *being*.[1]

A woman may say "I love you" by touching, stroking, caressing, and talking.

A man, on the other hand, shows love by doing such things as going to work and earning a living.

When a woman thinks about love, she thinks about starlit nights and romantic interludes. When a man thinks about love, he thinks about bringing home enough money to buy spaghetti sauce to put on the table.

A woman wants to be swept off her feet, while a man may think sweeping the front porch does just that.

Women feel. Men do.

We were hung up on these differences for years. "Why can't you show me you love me? I need to *feel* loved," we'd say.

And our husbands would respond, "What in the world does that mean? What can I *do* to make you *feel* loved?"

Notice that our husbands asked what they could *do* to make us *feel* loved? They had no idea what we meant because doing is a man's native tongue while feeling is a woman's.

Countless articles and books have been written describing these fundamental differences, yet it wasn't until we actually began to take this difference into consideration that we began to notice the ways in which our husbands express love.

Before learning this, when I (Connie) would say to my husband, "I need you to make me *feel* loved," my husband would respond, "I don't know how to do that if I haven't done it already. They didn't teach that in school, and if they did I was absent that day."

"It is not a hard thing to do," I would retort. And it's not—to a woman. But to a man it is like trying to read a map with no legend.

At some point my weary husband would say, "Besides making you *feel* cherished, what else can I *do?*"

What else? What else was there? Nothing—at least as far as I was concerned. I know now that what he was doing all those years was trying to give me exactly what I wanted. He was just doing it in a man's language. Imagine that!

Acknowledge the fact that you and your husband show love in entirely different ways, and appreciate your differences. Begin to look for the ways he shows love that are unique to him. One of the clues is that they will often be action based rather than feeling based.

For example, I (Connie) have learned that Wes shows love by supporting me in whatever I'm involved with, working hard to provide for me and our children, forgiving quickly, and not pressuring me to do things I don't enjoy. For instance, I don't enjoy cooking, and he doesn't make me feel bad that I don't. He's happy to eat whatever I prepare. It's usually very simple, but he always thanks me for preparing it.

My (Nancy) husband, Ray's, love language is seldom verbal. He's not a big hand-holder, either. However, he excels in demonstrating his love by doing things for me. If he has a day off and I'm working, he often cleans the house and has dinner ready when I get home. He calls me every day at work to see if I need anything from the store. As I first wrote these words, I heard him pull into the driveway after getting his car washed. I was ready to greet him, only to watch him pull out of the driveway in my car to have it washed. Knowing that I have a deadline to meet, he told me if I needed any errands run or household tasks completed, he was ready, willing, and able. I've learned that I don't need *words* when everything he *does* lets me know he loves me.

When you begin to accept your husband's efforts, you are granting him the uncommon luxury of being himself. What would happen if women stopped expecting men to be more like them? We think one of the first things that would happen is that husbands would feel freer to talk.

Bottom Line: Men express love by doing. They are action based rather than feeling based.

chapter two

MEN DON'T WORRY, FRET, OR FUSS

Men don't show their love by worrying, fretting, or fussing over someone like women do. They are too busy mowing the lawn, changing the oil, or caulking the air draft around the window. In fact, this is their way of fussing.

They don't wring their hands and wonder if you are okay if it is raining outside when you are driving home. There's nothing they can *do* about the rain, so what good is it to worry? Women, on the other hand, are expert worriers and worry until either the rain stops or their loved ones arrive home safely. Their worrying seems to be attached to the way they love, even though the worrying serves no purpose and adds nothing to life.[1]

A few years ago, a good friend of ours took her children to visit her parents. On the return trip they encountered an unexpected snowstorm. Traveling was perilous, and she debated whether to stop or go on. She decided to continue. Mile by mile she made her way home. She was exhausted when she pulled into her driveway, and every muscle in her body ached with tension.

She went running into the house to assure her husband that she and the kids were safe. She found him in their bedroom, watching television.

"Honey, we're home, and we're safe!" she exclaimed.

"I'm glad," he responded, giving her a hug and then hugging the kids.

She waited on him to "fuss" over her a bit. He didn't. He asked about the trip and whether they had had fun at her parents'. This baffled her. Surely in just a minute he would tell her how worried he had been and how brave she was. This, however, was not forthcoming.

Finally, she asked, "Were you worried?"

"No," he replied. "You have such common sense—I knew that if the roads were bad you'd pull over, and if they weren't, you'd make it just fine. I trust your judgment completely."

Somehow his response seemed so anticlimactic! She suddenly wished her sense wasn't quite so common. She was disappointed and hurt that he hadn't been glancing out of the window every few minutes to see if they were safely home. She knew not to ask if he'd been pacing or if he'd called the highway patrol to check out road conditions. Worry? What worry?

It didn't mean he loved her less because he didn't worry—it just meant he showed his love differently than she would have given the same circumstances.

Bottom Line: Don't expect cats to bark, sheep to moo, or husbands to worry, fret, or fuss.

chapter three

HIS PERSONALITY IS DIFFERENT FROM YOURS

Why is it so often that after the honeymoon, women put their husbands' personalities under a microscope and after careful examination reach the conclusion that something is wrong with their personalities?

We were both guilty of this and realized that we needed to recapture the love we felt for our husbands earlier in our marriages. We discovered that one way to do this was to focus on our husbands' positive qualities. It helped us to think about what drew us to our husbands in the first place.

My (Nancy) husband is direct, blunt, and goes straight to the point. I loved this about him when we met as I have a tendency to wrap my opinion in flowers—to the point that sometimes people aren't sure what I mean. You never have to wonder with Ray. Not long after we were married, though, I began to see this as a negative, and I set about to change this irritating little habit of his.

I discovered, after many years of marriage, that this "little habit" was not a habit at all, but part of my husband's personality! In their book *The Two Sides of Love* Gary Smalley and John Trent liken personalities to animals. I didn't know when I got married that I was marrying a "lion"—one who is strong, bold, and has a "let's get this done now" approach. And surely he didn't know he was marrying an "otter"—one who does things with excellence but likes to have fun doing them.

Do you see what happened? What I had once considered a fine character trait, I now thought of as a huge thorn in my side.

This occurs frequently in marriage. What was once seen as generosity is now seen as wasteful. Or perhaps you once thought your man was prudent but now consider him stingy. Maybe you loved his attention to detail when you were dating, but now you see him as compulsive and rigid.

I (Connie) liked that my husband always strove for excellence in whatever he did. If he skied, he jumped off cliffs. If he studied, he aimed for the highest grade. If he swam, he swam seventeen miles. Being more laid back, I found this amazing, and I loved it about him. I was his most ardent fan. Then we were married, and I was considered a bona fide member of his Shoot for the Stars club.

For example, shortly after our wedding he asked me, "What do you want to do with your life?"

I didn't know for sure what he meant. "Just live it, I guess," I told him.

"What else?" he asked.

What else? I didn't know. "I plan on working until we have children." That sounded like a good answer to me.

"Then let's talk about your career. What do you want to do in your field?"

What did I want to do? I was an occupational therapist, and I thought all was well—I had a challenging job and made a good living.

"Do you want to write a book about innovative therapy?" he suggested.

"Not particularly."

"Do you want to do research on the side?"

"Absolutely not. I'm not a research person."

"Do you want to develop a new splint?" he offered.

"No, I'm not a splint person either."

"You mean your mind isn't constantly whirling with ideas for splints that have never been invented?"

"No," I replied, "not a single whirl."

"Then what? Surely you don't want to be just a normal therapist?"

I was happy as a clam being a "normal therapist"! Suddenly his quest for excellence didn't seem nearly so fun now that I was a part of it. It took us years to appreciate each other's unique makeup in this regard.

Here is a lighthearted way to identify traits you or your husband might possess. This is from *The Two Sides of Love* by Gary Smalley and John Trent.[1] Try using these descriptions to help you reflect on what attracted you to your mate in the first place.

Are you a lion? A lion takes charge and is determined, assertive, firm, enterprising, and competitive. A lion enjoys challenges and is bold and purposeful. A lion is also a decision maker, a leader, goal driven, self-reliant, and adventurous. A lion says, "Let's do it now!"

Or are you an otter? An otter takes risks and is a visionary, a motivator, and a promoter. An otter is also very verbal and energetic, avoids details, is fun loving, likes variety, enjoys change, and is creative. An otter is group oriented, mixes easily, and is optimistic. An otter says, "Trust me! It'll work out!"

Maybe you are a beaver: deliberate, controlled, reserved, predictable, practical, orderly, and factual. A beaver is discerning, detailed, analytical, inquisitive, precise, persistent, and scheduled. A beaver says, "How was it done in the past?"

Finally there is a golden retriever, who is loyal, undemanding, and even keeled. A golden retriever tends to avoid conflict, enjoys routine, dislikes change, forms deep relationships, and is adaptable, sympathetic, thoughtful, nurturing, patient, tolerant, and a good listener. "Let's keep things the way they are," a golden retriever says.

Recognize that each personality type has its own strengths and weaknesses. Endeavor to maximize your husband's strengths and minimize his weaknesses. Many of your differences will soften over time and won't seem as glaring to you as they do right now.

Try to make it a daily habit to think on the qualities that drew you to your mate. You'll soon begin to see him in a completely different light as you train your mind in this new way. You may find your love for your husband renewed as you do this.

Personality? Yes! His personality plus your acceptance makes for a great combination.

Bottom Line: Say hello to a fresh way of looking at your husband's personality.

chapter four

MEN LOVE SOLUTIONS

Because men are goal oriented, they love finding solutions, and they especially love finding solutions to *your* problems. It can be frustrating to a woman when her husband tries to solve her problem as she's speaking, when all she really wants him to do is listen to her.

Simply talking about a problem makes no sense to a man. But discovering a solution—now there's a goal worth pursuing! Men don't usually talk just to talk. They talk when something is on their minds or when a problem needs to be solved. Women, on the other hand, develop relationships by talking. They bond with people and get to know them better through their verbal skills.

A problem doesn't have to be resolved in order for a woman to feel she's made progress—simply being heard is progress. But for a man it does. This difference can drive a woman crazy. But if you can begin to understand that this is one of the ways a man shows love, then it can seem almost sweet that he's trying to help you in this way. Because that is his intention—*to help you.*

Not long ago a friend of ours went to great lengths to prepare a special meal for her family. Unfortunately, due to an unanticipated phone call and a child needing to be taken somewhere, she forgot about the meat in the oven and it burned.

She was very disappointed. She had spent a lot of time on the meal and more money than usual on the meat. Her husband came through the door and asked what the odor was in the air.

"I burned the meat," she explained somewhat dejectedly and told him briefly what had happened.

"You either need to learn to use the automatic timer or not leave the house when the meat is cooking," he said. "Where's the instruction book? I can teach you how to use the timer right now."

The oven didn't have an automatic timer, and she didn't really want his helpful suggestions. All she wanted was a sympathetic ear. However, men aren't into sympathetic listening; they are into fixing problems.

When you would like to have your husband listen without offering a solution, say to him, "Most wonderful man in the world, could you do me a big favor? I need to talk to someone. Could I talk to you? I don't want you to solve my problem or tell me what to do. All I want you to do is listen to me. You don't have to say a word; just nod your head occasionally, and squeeze my hand a time or two. Would you do that?"

Since he knows up front that his problem-solving skills aren't going to be needed, he can turn that section of his brain off and simply listen to you. Granted, he may listen a little less actively than you'd like, but he'll still listen. He can't remotely imagine why you'd rather *not* have his valuable, problem-solving input, but since you made it clear from the beginning that listening is what you would like, he'll agree to your terms.

After he does this—listens without trying to solve your problem—thank him profusely. Make a big deal of it, because it is a big deal. "You are such a great listener! Thank you for listening to me—I know you have a million other things to do. You are my knight in shining armor. I feel so much better."

Now you're validating him for what he did, even though he is not sure what good it served. But men like being validated, and they like making their wives feel better, too. Suddenly he feels chivalrous. How long has it been since he has felt like that?

He'll begin to see, in a backdoor sort of way, that he did help to solve your problem—that your countenance is brighter and your mood has lifted. He'll begin to think that maybe this listening business isn't such a bad thing after all!

Bottom Line: Solving your problems is one way your husband says "I love you."

chapter five

YOU SPEAK DIVERSE LOVE LANGUAGES

Men and women don't often speak the same love language. Recognizing how your husband's love language differs from yours will greatly enhance communication in your marriage.

This thought is expounded upon in a great little book written by Gary Chapman called *The Five Love Languages*.[1] In it he lists five love languages that men and women speak:

1. Words of affirmation
2. Quality time
3. Gifts
4. Acts of service
5. Physical touching

If you speak Language number one and your husband speaks Language number five, sooner or later you're going to encounter some major problems in your communication—probably sooner! One of the best things you can do to enhance the emotional climate of your marriage is to understand which love language your husband speaks.

I (Connie) didn't know about this concept for years, and as a result, we spent many years speaking without communicating—not to mention the long stretches where we didn't speak at all.

My love language is words of affirmation. I wanted my husband to tell me how much he loved me—to whisper in my ear how wonderful I was. I used to take his hand as we drifted off to sleep and tell him I loved him. I sometimes wondered why he didn't return the gesture more frequently, and one day I asked him.

"If I'm trying to get to sleep, I'm not thinking about holding your hand," he said. Ouch! That hurt my feelings and seemed insensitive. But he's a goal-oriented man, and his goal was to get to sleep, not to hold my hand. Furthermore, his love language is acts of service, not words of affirmation or physical touch.

I could take his hand and tell him I loved him until I was 102, but he would far rather I:

- pick up his dry cleaning on time,
- keep fruit on hand,
- hem his new pants (I hate to sew),
- remove all my "stuff" from his car.

My (Nancy) husband and I lived similarly. Like Connie, my love language is also words of affirmation; but it is not my husband's. He felt no need to tell me that he loved me. He had already told me at least twice—when we became engaged and when we were married. He felt that was enough. In his mind, this issue had been dealt with. Why would I need reassurance?

But what I wanted was verbal affirmation of his love. Since this rarely occurred, I would go fishing for it. I often went overboard in telling him how much I loved him, hoping, I suspect, that it would cue him to do the same. This made him very uncomfortable. No matter what I did, I couldn't seem to prime that verbal pump. It was simply a nonissue with him—unnecessary and unneeded. He didn't need verbal affirmation to know I loved him and couldn't understand why I didn't feel the same way.

His love language is acts of service. Now I know what says "I love you" to Ray:

- a clean house,
- taking care of the wash and putting it away,
- making our evenings comfortable and relaxing,
- reading the paper with him in the morning,
- surprising him with a sweater from his favorite men's store.

Having realized and even coming to appreciate his love language, I no longer go fishing.

If your husband is constantly bringing you gifts for no particular reason, most likely gift giving is his love language. Since opposites generally attract, this is probably not your love language, and if you are extremely practical, you may even see his efforts as a waste of money. But can you begin to see that what's he's really saying is "I love you"? You just haven't been hearing it until now.

Study your husband, and see just what it is that makes him feel loved. Whatever you discover, begin to practice it. Don't announce what you are doing, and avoid the temptation to keep track of who does what for whom.

Not long ago we had a young wife ask for our input regarding what she should do for her husband, whom she was "kidnapping" from work a few hours early on a Friday afternoon.

We asked her what he liked to do, and she said he enjoyed going to the movies. So we suggested that she take him to the movies as part of their adventure.

"Oh, no," she replied. "I'm not going to take him to the movies—I don't like the movies."

Do you get the point? Sometimes we only want to do what we like to do, rather than thinking of our husbands and what they enjoy. Try thinking about him and what says "I love you" in his love language. You might be surprised at the outcome.

Bottom Line: Become bilingual—speak both your love language and his love language fluently.

chapter six

MEN DON'T LISTEN THE WAY WOMEN DO

Now there's an understatement! One thing that was helpful to us as we dissected this issue of communication in marriage was to recognize the differences in the ways in which men and women listen.

First of all, a woman tends to give verbal and visual cues to show she's listening. She frequently says things like "yes," "I see," "you're kidding," or something along those lines. She might nod her head or widen her eyes in surprise to let the person who's speaking know she's listening to every word.

If a woman told her friend that she'd seen a three-headed monster on the way to the grocery store, the friend would squeal and say, "What? Are you serious? What did you do?" She might even pat her chest as she spoke, as if to calm a racing heart. Her mouth would undoubtedly fly open, and her eyes would be as wide as saucers.

Men do not react this way. If a woman said the same thing to her husband, he'd most likely say nothing and wait for her to finish speaking. There would be no breathlessness, no squealing, no jumping up and down, and certainly no heart palpitations. In fact, he might look downright bored.

Verbal and visual cues are simply not part of how men typically respond.

The best way to know that your husband is listening to you is to ask for a few minutes of his time before speaking. You could say something like, "The funniest thing happened to me today, would you like to hear about it?" Realize that he may say no, or perhaps, "Not right now."

Another indication that he is listening is if he stays in the area where you are speaking. He may sit and look at you while you talk but with little change in expression—but he is probably listening.

This leads us to our second point. Men usually want "just the facts, ma'am." While women relish talking about the details of a situation, men do not necessarily enjoy listening to them. They prefer it short, sweet, and to the point.

Early in our marriage, I (Nancy) would start to tell my husband something and he might say, "Is this going to take very long?" This used to upset me to no end! My feelings would get hurt, and I would go into my quiet mode. Ray could never understand why I was so upset.

My (Connie) husband behaved similarly, frequently asking, "Should I get comfortable?" after I had begun to share something with him. I thought this was rude and usually stopped in the middle of my story to tell him so.

Neither of our husbands intended to hurt our feelings. They were simply trying to find out whether our stories were going to be a quick sprint or the Boston marathon.

We were hurt when our husbands asked us questions because we would never dream of doing the same thing to them. It took us years to understand that they were "just the facts" kind of men, as most men are. If your husband is like this, learn to get to the point quickly. Save the details for your friends.

Third, although men in general are single-task folks, *listening seems to be the one area at which they become multitask*! A woman might be telling her husband something, and the next thing she knows he is out in the garage rummaging around for a tool of some sort. She raises her voice and continues and, sure enough, soon he comes back in the kitchen, tool in hand.

As she's working her way to the main point of her story, she notices that he's now pulling the refrigerator away from the wall and peering into its back like a skilled surgeon. She is so fascinated by this that she gets off track with her story. By now, her husband is on his knees, looking for a screw to tighten or an axle to grease. She is finally getting to the exciting point of her story, and all she can see are his feet sticking out from behind the refrigerator. She delivers the punch line in Oscar-winning style, and there is silence from the other side of the fridge. She repeats it, this time more loudly. He stands up, hoists the refrigerator back into place, rubs his hands together, and smiles at her. "That's nice, honey," he says. She's not sure if he's talking about her story or the back of the refrigerator.

It's our unproven theory that because they are *doers,* it's easier for men to listen if they're doing something in addition to listening. If your husband is like this, it may begin to wear on you over time. If you say anything to your husband about it, he'll likely be dumbfounded. After all, he was listening to you *and* he fixed the refrigerator—something you'd wanted him to do for a long time.

What to do with your "just the facts" man? Here are a few pointers.

1. Realize that men by and large don't want to know every detail. They want to know the bottom line. My (Nancy's) husband still says to me when I begin a story, "Is this going to take long?"
2. Understand that men hear the first two or three sentences and then begin to tune out. Say what you need to say in the first couple of sentences, and leave it at that. Save the wonderful details for women friends who'll appreciate them as much as you do!
3. If there's something that's going to require a significant amount of his time and attention, ask him if you could go out for bagels

and coffee that night (or the following morning, or whenever) and talk about it.

Here are a few suggestions for when your husband doesn't seem to be listening to you.

1. Pick your time wisely. You know his routine—if he's on his way out the door, has a big meeting, or is stressed, don't expect him to listen. In these situations, if he appears to be listening, he's probably just being polite.
2. If it has been a while since you had a meaningful conversation, make it your goal to begin with miniconversations that are upbeat and lighthearted.
3. Save unpleasant news until after he has been home for thirty minutes. Even better, wait until after he has eaten.
4. If it is a life-and-death matter, skip the first four points and tell him immediately.

Bottom Line: Unless he says otherwise, less is more to your husband.

chapter seven

HE NEEDS PROCESSING TIME

"How did you like the movie?" a friend of ours asked her husband.

"I don't know," he said. "I'd have to see it again to know how I liked it."

"Let me put it a different way then," she responded. "When you left the theater, were you thinking *That was a good movie,* or were you thinking, *That wasn't a very good movie?*"

"I wasn't thinking either. I was thinking that I need to see it again."

This banter shows another of the core differences between men and women: They process things differently. Women are processing as they speak and reach a bottom line very quickly, while men frequently don't speak until things are processed and don't get to the bottom line as fast.

Unless you understand this, you'll most likely become frustrated, annoyed, and even tempted to shut down your efforts to communicate with your husband. A woman may see this lack of a quick response as unkind and take it personally, when what her husband is really saying is, "I need time to think this through."

It is not unusual for a woman to ask her husband's opinion on something only to have him not respond immediately.

"What do you think about increasing the children's allowances?" she might ask.

No response.

She repeats the question. "What do you think?"

"I'm thinking," he finally says.

A few minutes later he has yet to respond—he is still mulling the matter over in his mind. She has already thought the issue through six times and has three options she'd like him to consider—narrowed from a list of eight. All the while, he continues to think about it.

A friend shared that it took her many years to understand this about her husband. He frequently networked with a number of people whom she knew. After each meeting she would ask him to tell her all about it, to which he'd reply, "I need some time to process everything before I'm ready to talk about it. I'll get back to you in a few days." This seemed cold and dismissive to her. Why could he not share a few simple details with her on the spot?

Early on in their marriage, she pressed him for details. This only served to frustrate him, and he grew less inclined to share anything at all with her.

She then began to openly question this processing time. After all, it was "just" a meeting. She wasn't asking for an in-depth report, just a few tidbits. But, it seemed, he wasn't into tidbits. She continued to press him for details and grew increasingly annoyed.

Finally, without realizing what she was doing, she found herself deriding him. She looks back now and is shocked at how harsh she was. "It was nothing for me to say something like, 'I know you had a meeting today. Maybe you can tell me about it in the next three to five years, if that fits into your schedule.'" Her husband, who had said little in the past, now said nothing.

If your husband is like this, try not to push him for details. Give him plenty of time to process things and get back to you, and try not to become frustrated. If you need his opinion on something, give him plenty of lead time before asking for a decision.

For instance you might say, "Honey, the kids have a break coming up the second week in March. I think it would be fun to take a short trip somewhere. Would you think about it? Maybe we could talk over this weekend."

Men love this kind of communication. There's a goal, a time frame, and no pressure to answer on the spot before they've had time to think things through.

Acknowledge that your husband's style of listening and processing may be different than your own, and accommodate to this. Learn to hold your tongue when you're tempted to make a sharp, biting, or judgmental remark. It will reap many rewards.

Bottom Line: Men need time to process.

chapter eight

WHAT'S OBVIOUS TO YOU ISN'T OBVIOUS TO HIM

One of the most frustrating things to a woman is that what may be obvious to her isn't to her husband. Even the most sensitive of husbands often miss what seems so blatantly obvious to their wives. Why? It seems to us that many women have a sense of intuition that men don't have. This isn't always the case of course but it seems to be a general fit in regard to most men and women. And this isn't to say that women are smarter or superior to men; it's simply to say that this is one of our many differences, and if left unrecognized it can become an emotionally charged issue in marriage.

For example, let's say you and your husband go out to eat with another couple—Bonnie and Jack. You immediately sense that something is not right between the two of them.

You mention this to your husband on the way home. He neither noticed nor sensed anything, and he tells you that he thinks you are way off base and are reading too much into things. You are certain that you aren't. Now things are not only tense between Bonnie and Jack; they are suddenly tense between you and your husband.

A few days later Bonnie calls and tells you that she and Jack are struggling in their marriage and asks if you can recommend a counselor. You aren't surprised, and can't wait to share the news with your husband. Why? Not because you are concerned about Bonnie and Jack, but to show your husband that your hunch was correct.

We recommend you not do this. Of course you can share the news with him, but do not do it in a smug "I was right and you were wrong" fashion, which is often a woman's first instinct. Remember that what is obvious to you isn't to him.

Years ago, my (Connie) husband and I moved to San Antonio. We bought a small home on Canterbury Hill and moved in shortly before my husband was to report for duty. He was a captain in the army at the time.

The house needed quite a bit of work, and my husband busied himself with a number of chores while I painted the kitchen cabinets. One afternoon I went out to the backyard to take a break from the paint fumes. As I walked around the yard, a woman called to me from the back fence. She lived on the block behind us and had seen me walking around the backyard. She barely gave me her name or said "Welcome" before she began telling me the unspoken rules of the neighborhood, concluding with the comment that we seemed like the kind of people who would be happy to abide by them. I found her behavior quite odd and suspected that she policed the neighborhood to see who was living by her rules. I also suspected that we had not heard the last of her advice.

My husband saw nothing unusual about her remarks and even thought that she was probably everyone's favorite neighbor. You probably know whose impression proved true! To this day, my husband wonders how I was able to read her so well. What is frequently obvious to a woman isn't to a man.

An excellent example of this occurred in the life of a friend of ours. Ross told us that one day his wife came to him with her bags packed. She said she needed a few days away to get her head together. They'd been married nineteen years at the time, and he had thought everything was fine. But it wasn't.

His wife explained to him that she was tired of carrying the emotional load of the family. She was depleted from being the primary investor in their relationship. She was exhausted from keeping all the balls in the air. They had three children whom they loved dearly, but it seemed to her that her life continued basically unchanged while she scrambled to cover everyone else's needs except her own. Simply put, she was tired of covering all the bases.

She was miserable in her marriage, and he thought things were just fine. What was obvious to her was complete news to him.

What's so amazing is that this man isn't macho, egotistical, or self-centered. He is thoughtful, sweet spirited, and sensitive. His wife's happiness meant the world to him, yet he had no idea that she was anywhere near the end of her rope. His utter obliviousness was a poignant reminder that men need help in understanding how we're feeling—*before* we pack our bags.

This difference goes beyond the intuitive; it will play into your life as a couple almost daily. For instance, it may be obvious to you that the wastepaper baskets need emptying and the garbage needs to be taken out. Doesn't your man see this? Most likely it hasn't yet registered in his mind. It's not obvious to him.

Or take another example. Perhaps some of the countertop laminate has come loose and sort of flaps every time you brush up against it. It's obvious to you that it needs to be fixed. Your husband may notice the flapping, but it doesn't truly register. The need isn't obvious to him.

It's very likely that your man could use your help in this area. He's not overlooking the obvious on purpose; it's just that his "glasses" don't see things the way yours do.

Men register things differently, often more slowly. Give your husband the benefit of the doubt, and help him to see what seems so obvious to you.

Bottom Line: What's plain as day to you isn't to him.

chapter nine

MEN STICK TO SINGLE TASKS

By and large, most men are single-task oriented (except when it comes to listening) while women are multitask oriented. For example, if a man is watching television, that is usually all he is doing. He might get out the shoe polish and try polishing his shoes between touchdowns, but if the action gets very intense, he will stop and concentrate on the football game.

A woman on the other hand rarely does anything singly. Being able to do many tasks at once is as much a part of her makeup as the color of her hair and eyes. While she's cooking supper she's helping someone with homework, teaching her preschooler the ABC's, monitoring whether the upstairs toilet is still filling with water, talking to a friend on the phone, or mentally balancing the checkbook. Sometimes she may be doing all of these things at once!

Because of this, it is sometimes difficult for a woman to understand just how single task men really are.

A common example of this is how men operate in the kitchen. When they cook, they cook. Most stand over the stove working on their creation until it's done and don't think of much else.

When a woman cooks, though, she usually washes the dirty

dishes while she's waiting on something to sauté, boil, or melt; wipes off the counter in between steps; sets the table while the rolls brown; and may even run outside and gather fresh flowers for a centerpiece. That's multitask. Men don't usually do this. They just stick to cooking. Loading the dishwasher, setting the table, and gathering flowers or anything else isn't on their minds.

When a man gets a phone call, he tends to stop what he's doing and just take the call, while most women will take the call while they continue on with their task—dressing the child, cutting vegetables for supper, or folding the laundry.

Observing your husband's ways, understanding them, and accepting them will help you to be less frustrated and more patient. This does wonders for the environment in your home and helps to make the climate optimal for good communication.

Bottom Line: Mr. Single was not intended to be Mr. Multi.

chapter ten

HE ISN'T LIKE YOU SPIRITUALLY OR EMOTIONALLY

Just as a man and woman are often different in their task orientation, they are also different in their emotional and spiritual makeup. Your spiritual gifts will not be his. And your emotional strengths may not be his either.

For instance, your spiritual gift may be mercy and your husband's administration. If you don't take this difference into consideration, you could come to view your husband as harsh and uncaring because he's not filling the needs of others like you are. Maybe a family in the church has experienced a tragedy, but he's not motivated to go by and visit like you are. If someone has lost a job, he may not network as hard as you to help fill it. Perhaps he's never called anyone on the phone to ask how they're doing since the death of a family member, while you're calling three or four times a week. The reason he's not? He's gifted differently. Administratively gifted people often zoom in on the task at hand rather than on people themselves.

It would be helpful for you to learn not only about your own spiritual makeup but about his as well. Observe ways that God has gifted him, and encourage him to use those gifts. You will find that he has his own way of doing things.

Don't hold his personality against him. If he's an introvert, that's okay. If he enjoys laughing at a party and you are quieter, enjoy the sound of his laughter. Allow him to be all that he was created to be.

If you are a morning person and he is a night owl, don't grumble or consider him lazy when he sleeps in later than you do. He was probably a night owl when you married him, and you liked it then! Learn to like it again. Stop weighing his talents and personality against yours and deciding that he's lacking. All of us tend to think our way is best. But all of us are wrong! God's way is best—and He is the one who created us each uniquely.

It may be that the qualities you are wishing were different in your husband are those very things that are meant to hone and chisel you into the jewel you were meant to become.

Bottom Line: Stop wishing your husband were different. If you were exactly the same, one of you would be unnecessary.

chapter eleven

MEN DON'T USE DETAILS THE WAY WOMEN DO

Have you ever had this happen? Your husband comes home and announces that your friends Tom and Sue just had their baby. He ran into Tom in the office parking lot, and Tom shared the big news. Your first question, of course, is whether they had a boy or a girl. Your husband scratches his head, furrows his brow, and says, "I'm not sure. I don't think Tom said, and I didn't ask. If he did say, I don't remember."

You ask about Sue: "How is she doing? Did she have any problems during delivery?"

Your husband looks at you as if you've just dropped in from another planet, "How in the world would I know the answer to that?" he asks in disbelief.

This is one of the biggest differences between men and women. Most men look at the big picture and skip the details, while it's the details that create the big picture for a woman. Because they're not detail oriented, men sometimes seem forgetful. The reality is that they're not all that forgetful—*they simply never register the information in the first place.*

For instance, if a baby isn't his, it doesn't matter to a man whether the sex is male or female. What matters is that the baby was born. Who needs details? The big picture speaks for itself.

For a woman, however, the sex of the baby is just the beginning. She wants to know the baby's weight, length, coloring, who she resembles, how much hair she has, whether it is curly or straight, and so on. And then she wants to know about the delivery, the predelivery, and the postdelivery. The picture simply isn't complete without the details.

She often fails to understand that her detail-driven nature is specific to her, not her husband.

This difference goes beyond what registers with a man. Another aspect of this is that men remember few details—unless it's about a sporting event—while women tend to remember many details.

This can create much conflict because remembering who said or did what can cause a simple disagreement to turn volatile. A woman will "bet the farm" that her husband said something, did something, or promised something that her husband can't remember anything about.

For example, let's say Mary and Dave are discussing his tendency to want to control things. Dave asks Mary to give him an example of this. She reminds him of a family reunion they attended months earlier.

"It was the middle of July, and the air conditioning went out just as we were getting ready to eat. It was so hot. I had on that pink blazer and my white pants. My shirt underneath was sleeveless, and the armholes were cut so deeply I remember thinking I didn't dare take off my blazer, even though it was stifling. Sweat was rolling down every crevice of my body. The big kids were out in the backyard playing croquet and my sister had just put her two little ones down for a nap. I was eating a piece of Aunt Naomi's pie, when you announced that it was time for us to go. Right then! I had a piece of pie in my mouth and about choked on it. I was so upset. You didn't ask me if I was ready to go or even give me a fifteen-minute warning. You insisted we leave right then. My mother wrapped my pie in foil so I could eat it later. You stopped the croquet game and told the kids to get in the car. And Jordan was winning, too."

Dave doesn't remember any of this, but what can he say to Mary, who apparently remembers it down to the last potato chip that was eaten?

An awareness of this difference will help you not to use your detail-loving makeup against your husband. You may not even realize that you do it. But let's face it: When push comes to shove, you can outremember your husband every time, and by virtue of this alone you can gain the upper hand.

What you're basically doing is using one of your inherent strengths against your husband. This leaves him in a weakened position simply because he's not detail oriented. Since he can't hold a candle to what's being thrown at him, he'll often concede by default.

You can even use his integrity against him in this area: He knows you remember details well and he doesn't. You know he won't pretend otherwise, so you continue to press the point. You may win the battle, but you'll lose the war because a man simply doesn't enjoy talking to a woman who throws details in his face at every turn.

Bottom Line: When you speak about men and details, you are talking about square pegs and round holes.

chapter twelve

MEN GO THROUGH SEASONS

Your husband's season of life has a lot to do with why he does the things he does. What characterizes his life at twenty-five won't be true at forty-five. And what he does at forty-five he probably won't do at sixty-five.

Twenty-something husbands tend to be supercharged, super-driven guys. They may not work as hard at the relationship as their wives. They are busy making their way in the world and moving up the career ladder.

The same is often true for thirty-somethings. They've managed to get one leg up the ladder; now they're jockeying to get both legs on it. You may still feel as though you're the primary depositor into your marriage.

Forty-somethings experience a time of reflection. They are still charged and invigorated, but they realize that they may not be the next president of the United States. They also recognize that life is about more than just them. This proves truer with each succeeding decade.

I (Connie) used to wonder why it was that women seem to become bitter with age, while men seem to age more softly. I wonder if this concept doesn't have something to do with it.

Men tend to refocus as they pass through the seasons of life. Many of their goals have either been reached or deemed unreachable, unworthy, or too costly. They begin to look at life through a different lens and see what's really important. And what do they find? Relationships.

They begin making overtures to their wives, trying to find a way to reconnect and start over. But unfortunately the overtures may now be rejected because these women, who invested heavily in the relationship early on and seemingly to no avail, have begun to withdraw. Ironically women may do this just as their husbands begin to do what they wanted all along: more investment in the relationship.

Patrick M. Morley puts it this way:

> When husbands find themselves standing among the barren trunks of autumn, their regrets roost, their energy drops, their ambitions shift, and their desire for more "relationship" grows.
>
> As he becomes more interested in building a deeper relationship with his mate, this comes as quite a shock to his wife, who, in his absence, has built a life of her own.
>
> He glances to his side and drinks long of his beloved wife. He sees her as he has never seen her before. He sees that she, too, is unsettled and vulnerable, and he longs to recover that which for so many years he set aside.[1]

If your husband has "set aside" certain years in your marriage, give him a second chance. Don't allow yourself to become bitter, and don't stop investing in your marital relationship. Keep your spirit soft and your love for your husband tender. We think you will find your efforts rewarded.[2]

What if your husband is in an early season? We believe that employing the strategies in this book will help you stay connected to your mate as well as make the best of his energetic, world-conquering years.

Bottom Line: Your marriage has many seasons. Be the sunshine in all of them.

chapter thirteen

YOU MARRIED A WARRIOR

Have you ever said to yourself, "Why does my husband act that way?"

Most women wonder from time to time why their men act the way they do.[1] If you want communication to flourish in your marriage, it is helpful to take into consideration some of the physiological intricacies of men.

Men are equipped with much more testosterone than women. This not only helps them be strong; it is also a reason for some of those manly personality traits that can be so puzzling to women.

A man surges with this "gasoline." It revs up his body with energy, strength, and sexual drive. This hormone profoundly affects physique, behavior, and mood. It affects body hair, upper body strength, and the ratio of muscle to fat, among other things.

Testosterone charges through the brain and is often a factor in hyperactivity in boys. In general, boys are often better at spatial tasks and girls at verbal tasks. Men are usually action oriented, blunt, direct, and to the point.

Have you ever had a conversation that went something like this?

"Darling," you say one Saturday, "what is on your agenda this afternoon?"

"I am not going shopping at a bunch of stores. I am going to watch football this afternoon!" your man replies.

At this point, you have forgotten all you knew about the differences between men and women and are thinking angrily to yourself, *I didn't say one word about shopping! I don't want to go shopping. We've never gone to a 'bunch of stores.' And furthermore....*

Your man, in the meantime, is charged up for the game. He has probably been looking forward to it the entire week. You think, *Why couldn't he just say, "The only thing on my agenda this afternoon is football. Do you want to watch it with me?"*

Here's the deal: Testosterone doesn't usually equate with sweetness, and it may often be the cause of caution and manners being thrown to the wind. It is not that men simply mean to be rude.

Which response sounds best to you?

- "I forgot Oklahoma/Nebraska (our favorite teams!) are playing today. That sounds like fun.... I think I'll watch with you!"
- "Have a great time! I have Gatorade in the fridge and popcorn in the pantry. I'm running a few errands. Maybe I'll pick up some fried chicken on the way home. I'll see you in a few hours."
- "You are always so rude! What is wrong with you anyway?"
- "Is football more important than I am?" (Warning: Don't ask this question!)

We think this type of conversation poses an opportunity to simply overlook the manner in which your husband's opinion was stated and recognize that guys are like that sometimes.

Bottom Line: When your husband responds like a man, don't hold it against him.

chapter fourteen

NOTHIN' SAYS LOVIN' LIKE SOMETHIN' FROM THE OVEN

Most men equate love with food. They seem to come equipped with some sort of radar invisible to the naked eye that senses the whereabouts of food or lack thereof.

If you want to start a conversation, ask your husband what he'd like to eat on Sunday. Or ask him to tell you what his favorite childhood foods were. A trip down the past menus of life is fodder for more than knowledge, especially if he has fond memories of his past.

My (Nancy) husband, Ray, grew up on a modest ranch in Texas. He was actually a cowboy when he was a teenager. He and his dad used to camp out under the stars as they drove their herd of steers from one feeding ground to another. Foremost on his mind on those occasions was: "What will we eat when we get home?"

His mom was a great cook and made plenty of food for her guys. A typical Sunday dinner was a sight to behold—roast beef, fried chicken, ham and string beans, mashed potatoes, macaroni and cheese, deviled eggs, fresh corn, tomatoes, green onions, jalapeno peppers, celery, banana pudding, and perhaps a pie and cake as well. Almost all of it would have come from their farm.

Therefore if Ray called me from his office asking what we were having for dinner in the early years of our marriage, quiche was not a good answer. He began to coin phrases like, "That is lady food! I don't like lady food."

My (Connie) husband is into healthy eating in a major way—almost as much as I am into eating chocolate! I grew up on a farm where we ate considerable amounts of red meat. My husband prefers eating only fish and chicken. I knew of about 250 ways to prepare hamburger when we were first married, but only one way to fix chicken—fried; and one way to fix fish—burned!

Over the years I have learned, however. Wes greatly appreciates the fact that I take his preferences into consideration when planning our family meals. Although food isn't what speaks love to him, the fact that I acknowledge his choices does.

The point goes beyond food preference—it is about taking care of your husband in a way that he understands. This may seem very shallow to us females. Food means something to men that we don't really understand. This mysterious truth makes it all the more important to take it into account.

Even Wes, who isn't really a food person, will say, "Are we snacking tonight?" if he doesn't see evidence of supper in progress. Snacking is just fine—which means eating cereal, fixing oatmeal or grilled cheese, or something else simple. Caring less about the actual food, he does seem to want to know what the plan is.

Likewise, a friend of ours reports that her husband really doesn't start to talk until the food issue is clarified. "What's for dinner?" is an important question—it paves the way for further conversation.

Our editor told us that the lesson on the importance of food to her husband was driven home to her shortly after their wedding. When reminiscing about their trip to North Carolina for their honeymoon, the highlight for her is the magical tour they took of the Biltmore Hotel with the thousands of tiny candles and luminaries that lit the lawn and hallways and its enchanting Christmas décor. What her husband remembers is searching the county for that special North Carolina barbeque he'd tasted in the past, his delight at finding the BBQ Inn the last night of their stay in Asheville, and pulling up to the door scarcely two minutes before closing—just in time to have a great meal! Nancy has a beautiful picture book of the Biltmore as a souvenir, and John—he has a book on North Carolina barbeque and all the places it is served in that part of the country!

We suggest that you begin thinking of cooking again if you have stopped. We realize that you aren't superwoman, but superman is hungry! You can learn to prepare meals that take little preparation time. There are also all sorts of new appliances that can help you make wonderful meals in a short amount of time.

This morning I (Nancy) got up while it was still dark. While I was fumbling around to find the light switch, Ray said, "Let's have those steaks for dinner tonight!"

And so we will. My cowboy is hungry.

Bottom Line: The old saying "The way to a man's heart is through his stomach" surely was written by a hungry man.

part two

More About Him

different strokes for different folks

My dad is a man and he needs food,
a warm bed, lots of Diet Coke,
the right kind of toothpaste, clean socks,
and I think he likes clean underwear, too.
And he likes chocolate gravy on Saturday morning.
Most of all, though, he needs Mommy to love him.

TAYLOR, 6

Ask a man what he needs, and he will probably stare off into space wondering where that question came from. If you persist, he will probably say, "Nothing. Everything is fine."

We think meeting a man's needs has a lot to do with the quality of your interaction with him. We want to encourage you to not only study your husband to see what his needs are but to strive to meet them. This section will give you some insight into this radical suggestion.

Enormous fortunes have been built on small amounts of money faithfully invested over time. The same is true of relationships. Your husband's sense of worth can be greatly enlarged by your reaction to him. The way you treat him, therefore, affects your own quality of life. There is an irrefutable principle in life that we all know but give little thought to: You get back what you give out.

There are few things more challenging and more rewarding than becoming a need-meeting woman in your man's life. If your husband is running on empty, or even if you are, watch what happens when you begin to invest in his stock. His emotional portfolio will begin to grow. Value him, and he will begin to feel valuable to you. As a married couple what affects one affects the other. You will begin to see the results in your own life, too. It doesn't take long.

chapter fifteen

SPELL R-E-S-P-E-C-T HIS WAY

The comedian Rodney Dangerfield has gotten a lot of mileage out of a running joke. He sprinkles his routine with the phrase, "I don't get no respect." He is also the one that interjects, "Take my wife—please!" It is all in fun, but that surely could be the heartfelt cry of men in America, especially in the last thirty years or so. More often than not, men are portrayed as buffoons in sitcoms and cartoon strips.

In recent years there has been a huge cultural shift in what women expect men to do and be. Because of this, men aren't as clear as they used to be about their identities and worth. Our church is presently offering a class on what it means to be a man in today's world. It is held at *6:15* on Friday *mornings*. Over three hundred men show up each week and the class continues to grow.

We believe that one of the biggest investments you can make in your husband's life is to respect him.[1] Respect is critical in a man's life, and most men place a higher value on being respected than they do on being loved. Certainly a man who feels valued and treasured by his wife will be unafraid to share his innermost thoughts. He'll know that his name, which she shares, is held gently in her hands and in her heart as well.

Respect means to consider with high regard and esteem. Even if at the present time you have lost respect for the *man* you married, you can begin by renewing respect for his title, *husband*.

There are many ways you can immediately introduce respect into your marriage.

- Speak to him with courtesy. Your tone of voice matters!
- Speak about him with high regard.
- Teach your children to respect their dad through your example.
- Give attention to his departure and his homecoming. Even though there is a whole section on this later in the book, we cannot stress this enough. There are mornings when I (Nancy) send Ray off to work (if he leaves before I do) with a rousing rendition of "Hail to the Chief," saluting him and telling him his "helicopter" is ready. This is not a daily occurrence. If it were, he'd grow weary of it. It does elicit a grin when it happens.
- Learn to honor his decisions even if they are difficult to agree with. (We are not talking illegal or immoral here.)
- Fix him meals. Even though I work, I fix Ray's breakfast, serving it on a tray that doubles as a place mat. It is usually cereal and a banana, but I serve him on our best china dish, with a bowl on top of that. He is worth our best.
- Greet him on the phone with an uplifting endearment. "Hello, sweetheart" or "Hello, treasure." He may not always seem worthy of such a greeting, but he is of great worth to God.[2]
- Treat him as you would an honored dignitary, and don't crowd him out of your schedule.
- See him as Christ sees him—as a man in progress, as God's own child.
- Pray for him. Pray that he would walk in a manner worthy of the Lord, to please Him in all respects. That he would bear fruit in every good work and increase in the knowledge of God.[3]

- Don't talk negatively about your husband's family. It shows a lack of respect for him as well. This will put a wedge in your relationship. If you have done this, apologize and ask for forgiveness.

There is a story told of a family of four. As a visitor was nearing her time to leave, the two daughters and their mother jumped to their feet and said they must prepare for the father's homecoming. The mother busily attended to her appearance, and the daughters tidied up. They spoke in glowing terms about the man who was about to enter the door. Out of curiosity, the visitor waited, eager to see the giant of a man they spoke of. Without further ado the door opened and a slight, balding, bespectacled man walked in and was immediately surrounded by his exuberant wife and children. The visitor was startled until she realized that this little threesome actually saw him as a giant.

Bottom Line: See your husband as the giant he wants to become.

chapter sixteen

ACCEPT HIM

Accepting your husband is like placing him under Niagara Falls during a heat wave instead of sending him off to the Sahara Desert. Niagara Falls is a great place to begin creating an environment for good communication in your marriage. If you want to escape the Sahara, the map for the way out is an easy one to follow: Begin by *lowering* your expectations of your husband while *raising* your level of acceptance.

Most women have no idea how much this means to a man. In a nutshell, it means everything. A home isn't really a home if those who live within its walls don't feel loved and accepted for who they are; it is simply a house.

Sometime during their marriage a wife will begin a small makeover project—her husband. She has the best intentions in the world. A little tweak here and a little fine-tuning there would make him even better than he already is. The cost is high, though. You'll end up with a husband who resists your every suggestion and who doesn't want to talk.

Unless your husband asks—and he probably won't—don't get involved with makeovers. Let him know you think he's wonderful just the way he is.

Accepting your husband invites him to become who he really is inside rather than who you want him to be.

As your husband starts to feel more and more accepted by you, he will begin to talk more. If he doesn't feel accepted his energies will be spent enduring and surviving.

Think for a moment about who it is that you enjoy talking with. It is someone that makes you feel loved and valued for who you are. This person doesn't constantly put you down and tell you how you should change. She doesn't imply in any way that you are not the person she thinks you should be. If she did, you would undoubtedly begin to share less and less. The people you open up to accept you as you are—warts and all. Why would this be any different for your husband?

If you want to get out of the makeover business, here are a few steps to consider:

- Tell your husband every day that you love him just the way he is. It's amazing how many women no longer tell their husbands how much they are loved. If you've stopped, begin again to do this.
- Don't be quick with correction, criticism, condemnation, or chiding. This can be so tempting because our store of knowledge (and opinions) is so deep. Hold those thoughts!
- Don't interrupt. Women are intuitive and react almost immediately to what's being said. A woman can think of six or eight responses to what her husband is saying before he's finished his original thought. If he is talking about a problem, most of us could tell him immediately what we would do in the same situation before he takes his first breath. Remember that men don't need or want our answers unless they ask for them.
- Similarly, resist the urge to cut to the chase when he's talking. Let him talk! He may wander all over the back forty acres when he could simply walk across the street to say the same thing, but there's value to be found in wandering the forty acres. Let

him find that value at his own pace. You may be a quicker thinker, but that doesn't mean you're a better thinker. It simply means you think differently.

- At the core of each of us is the longing to be accepted. It only makes sense that there is no one our husbands would more desire to be accepted by than us.[1]

Bottom Line: Acceptance isn't just the bow on the gift—it is the gift.

chapter seventeen

EMBRACE THE POWER OF APPRECIATION

Do you know what motivates a man? It is appreciation, pure and simple.

Think how the following words would make your husband feel.

"You are so wonderful. The lawn looks great. Thanks for mowing it earlier than usual so it will look nice for my get-together tonight.

"Thank you for handling that sticky situation with your aunt. You showed such wisdom and discretion in what you said. You do such a great job in these situations. I appreciate it.

"Thanks for listening to me tonight. I was so discouraged and worried, but you made me feel so much better just by listening to me talk about it."

Appreciation is fuel for a man. It motivates him to want to do more, just as lack of it will cause him to want to do less. This is also true of communication. If all you do is needle and harangue your husband about talking to you, just the opposite will occur. But if you want to increase your husband's conversational skills, we suggest you appreciate what he does in this area already.

The next time your husband shares something with you (no matter how small, and we know it might be minuscule), say to him,

"Thank you so much for sharing that with me. I enjoy knowing what has gone on in your day."

And then leave it at that! What often happens is that many women can't leave it at that. They go on to say something like, "I wish you'd tell me about your day more often. I'm home with the kids all day and need to talk to someone besides a two-year-old."

Her husband is thinking, "Oh no, give her an inch and she'll take a mile." The safest thing for him to do is not even offer the inch.

But when you appreciate his sharing and don't pressure him for more, that feels kind of good to a guy. "Hmm," he's thinking. "What a guy! I seem to have caused my wife much happiness. And it wasn't even that big of a deal. I wonder what would happen if I talked to her a little more…maybe I will."

And when he does, say the same thing: "Thank you for telling me about that! It just makes my day for you to share those things with me. You are so sweet to be considerate of me in that way."

"Considerate?" he's thinking. "Wow, she just said I was considerate. I like the sound of that. I like being considerate. She seems so appreciative, and she's not nagging me about how I need to talk to her more. Maybe I'll give her two inches next time instead of just one."

And when he does, you know what to say! In a sense, you're causing him to see himself in a whole new light. He's gracious. He's considerate. He's kind. *He's conversational!* It just makes your day, and you tell him so. What you are doing is making it easy for him to talk by removing the hoops he has always had to jump through in the past.

One word of warning as he begins to share with you: Don't put him down in any way for what he says, how he says it, or what he's talking about. You may not care the least bit about motorcycles, but if you want him to keep talking to you, get interested fast! If he uses an incorrect word or the wrong tense of a verb, let it go. If he gets little facts turned around, leave them be. Set him up for success.

This principle works in the home as well. Find something that he already does for you, and tell him you appreciate it. We cannot tell you how much he'll love this, and it opens the door to his wanting to do more. If he takes the baby on a walk around the block, thank him profusely. Your generosity sparks his. You'll make him sound like such a wonderful man that he'll want to become even more like the man about whom you are speaking.

Bottom Line: Appreciation and a husband's motivation go hand in hand.

chapter eighteen

BEGIN TO SAY "THANK YOU"

Dr. John Gottman reports that long-lasting, "in love" marriages enjoy a regular quantity of five positive experiences to one negative.[1] How are you doing in this regard? Is your husband thirsty for a positive comment from your lips? If he is, give him a drink! Or two. Or five![2]

Just last night a friend told us how she was packing boxes, preparing for a move to Minnesota. As she packed each box—memory upon memory—she realized what a wonderful life she'd had in Omaha for the past several years. She said it caused her to feel exceedingly thankful for her hard-working, faithful husband.

So she got on the phone and without pretense or further ado simply said, "Thank you for the wonderful life you've given me in Omaha. Thank you for working hard and being so faithful to the kids and me." Her husband was stunned. For several moments the phone line remained silent—he was completely taken aback. It was then, she told us, that she realized how little he'd heard the words *thank you* from her in almost thirty years of marriage. She was grieved.

She then asked herself if she'd ever said thank you to her parents for her wonderful childhood. No, she didn't think that she had. So she went home and called them and said, “Mom and Dad, you gave me a great life as a child. Thank you.” Her parents reacted as her husband had.

This is not the stuff of daily conversations. But it should be! Make thankfulness a part of your life. You will see your husband blossom virtually before your eyes.

Keep in mind that if you have not made a habit of letting your husband know that you are thankful for him, much of what you say in simple daily conversation may be taken by him as criticism, whether you mean it that way or not. What we are saying is, if he has gone for an extended time with very little or no gratitude, his spirit begins to close and harden toward you. He goes into what our husbands call “survival mode.” Realizing that there is very little oxygen (verbal thankfulness) in the air, he begins to eke out an existence apart from you.

It saddened us to realize that our husbands lived this way for far too long. We had no idea how important this was to a man. We knew respect was important, but we didn’t know gratitude was. It is of utmost importance, and it is really a very simple thing.

One of the most overlooked areas is telling your husband how thankful you are that he earns a living. Even if you work as well, his hard work is something to be grateful for. Most men work hard to provide for their families, and it is music to a man’s soul to have you acknowledge it (even if he doesn’t reciprocate). Words like this are profound to a man and can make huge inroads into tearing down the wall of silence in a marriage.

Other areas you might consider are:

- his consideration for parents and family,
- his readiness to help a friend,
- his willingness to spend time with the kids (don’t let the idea that this is something he “should” do get in the way),
- his helping around the house,
- his timeliness,

- his grooming,
- his integrity,
- his sense of humor,
- his thoughtfulness regarding intimacy.

Bottom Line: Thank you. These are two words that bless the hearer and should tumble from your lips daily.

chapter nineteen

MEN LOVE TO BE ADMIRED

Acceptance and appreciation have hopefully eliminated much of the rust on the hinges of the door to communication, and it has now begun to swing open. Admiration gives it a big push like nothing else does! It is a unique, intimate thing that encourages his sharing.

The fact is that men like being admired. If you doubt this, tell him you love him and watch his response. Then share with him something you admire about him. Say to him, "There is something about you that I admire greatly," and tell him what it is. Watch his attentiveness now! You will see that you have his full attention. Even the football game he was so interested in may fade into the background as he waits to hear what it is you admire. That's how powerful words of admiration are to a man.

In many marriages admiration is on the verge of extinction, but a wife who is willing to reintroduce it into her marriage can bring it back to a thriving, flourishing state.

As you begin to do this, your husband might at first be surprised. This may be a drastic change for him, and he may well be shocked—great! When a battery is dead, do you know what you do? You shock it. And it often comes to life again. You may begin to see signs of life in your husband that have long been dormant simply by sharing something you admire about him.

I (Nancy) learned years ago the powerful impact admiration has on a husband. After hearing about it, I decided to see if it was true. Ray had just come into the kitchen, and I caught a glimpse of his arms. He had been mowing the yard, and his arms were glistening with sweat. He is used to working hard and has strong, muscular biceps. I asked him to make a muscle for me. I thought he might think this was silly, but he thought it was a wonderful idea and immediately volunteered! Later that day, when he was in the backyard and saw me looking out the window at him, he stopped what he was doing, flexed his arm, and made a muscle. I was smiling from ear to ear as I watched him, and so was he.

This kind of warmth has not always been part of our marriage. Those were the days before I had made a commitment to Christ or owned a Bible.[1] I hadn't realized that God's Word had much to say about how to live my life as a wife. Before that, admiring my husband was the last thing on my mind, and talking to me was the last on his. Admiration was one of those things that began the rekindling process.

There are a number of ways you can begin to admire your husband. It means something to a man to be admired for his character. Is your husband hard-working, honest, kind? Is he a man of integrity and uncompromising principles? If he is, tell him what you notice about him.

Admire something about his physique—do his eyes sparkle? Do you love his work-worn hands? Is his smile especially nice? Men don't mind it a bit when you admire their physical attributes. Admire his lovemaking skills. Without going into detail, suffice it to say that men especially love this!

True admiration is an intimate thing and gives a man a sense of security. It is so powerful, though, that you must use caution to assure that your motives are pure and that there are no self-serving purposes attached. For example, don't admire him to "soften him up" because you want something from him. Admire him because he is your husband and holds a place of honor in your heart and home.

Bottom Line: Admiration is like a cold drink of water to a thirsty man.

chapter twenty

SMILE!

"A cheerful look brings joy to the heart."[1]

A smile is a great way to show love to your husband. Smile at him when you see him. After all, who wants to talk to a sourpuss? This is one of the things we teach in our Bible study. We encourage women to go home and look in the mirror in the same way they look at their husbands. Have you done that lately?

Connie has a very expressive face. She smiles all the time, even when she's talking. I (Nancy) remember her demonstrating to our class the look she had seen in the mirror several years before when viewing her everyday expression toward Wes. We roared with laughter. Where was her smile? Why was her brow furrowed? Why was her jaw set? I'd never seen her purse her lips like that, or for that matter scrunch up her eyes. Neither had she! She related that she was shocked at the apparition Wes saw day after day. After only one glimpse of how she looked, Connie purposed to change her expression, and she has. Wes now beholds the joyful face her friends and her children see.

Begin to notice facial expressions. Watch people looking at babies or Christmas trees. Notice how soft their faces look.

Become more aware of how you are looking at your husband. Men hate those "looks" we give them, sometimes without even realizing it. Work at ensuring that the look he sees is one of love.

Bottom Line: Your face is your front door. Is it wreathed in a smile?

chapter twenty-one

PUT THE WIND BACK IN HIS SAILS

In his book *What Husbands Wish Their Wives Knew about Men,* Patrick Morley says:

> If I could make only one observation about men today, it would be that men are tired—mentally, emotionally, physically, and spiritually tired. Weary of life. When I make this observation at our men's seminars it evokes as much response as anything else I say. Many heads nod in agreement while others droop to their chests.[1]

Mr. Morley has spoken to hundreds of men, and this is the issue that seems to hit home the hardest—their need for encouragement. It can be so easy for women to forget their husbands need this; we assume they are getting plenty of encouragement at the office. But "at the office" encouragement just isn't the same as "in the home" encouragement. And the best "in the home" encouragement that exists is the encouragement that comes from a loving spouse.

I remember my (Connie) husband coming home from work one

day. I sensed his day had been difficult when he came through the door, though he didn't say a word. Perhaps it was the slump of his shoulders or the sigh that escaped his lips. My warrior was weary.

When warriors are weary, they need to be encouraged. I don't remember what I said or did, but I do remember that later that night my husband thanked me for encouraging him. This was a big deal to me because in prior years I might have rolled my eyes and asked him why he was so tired. It's so much better to put the wind in your husband's sails than put in a rip that deflates the sails completely.

A friend told us recently that her husband had gone to work at a car dealership. After the first few weeks on the job, his manager approached him and handed him a hundred-dollar bill. "I've noticed what a great job you're doing," he said. "Keep up the good work."

The woman said it was as if someone had given him a prized possession—he was so excited. Certainly he didn't mind the extra money, but even more it was clear that what meant so much to him were the encouraging words.

If you want your husband to talk to you, start being an encourager to him. An encourager is one who gives strength, one who gives courage. You may find that your husband's heart softens towards you as you encourage him. It is one of a man's deepest needs.

Do you need to become more of an encourager to your husband? Do a quick check to see how you're doing in this area:

- How often do you say, "You can do it! I believe in you! You're the best!"?
- How often do you notice his effort to make the yard look nice or to keep the cars running smoothly?
- When was the last time you said, "You handled that situation so well"?
- Do you acknowledge when he's going through a difficult time and let him know you're there for him?
- Is your home a place your husband enjoys returning to every night?

- Are you a chronic complainer?
- Do you look for opportunities to compliment him on his wisdom?

As one man told us, "When my wife encourages me, I feel like there's nothing I can't do! There's no mountain I can't climb or problem I can't solve. I'm the man! I'm *her* man! Nothing reenergizes a man like a little encouragement from his wife."

Bottom Line: Encouragement is to the soul what spinach is to Popeye.

chapter twenty-two

YOUR HUSBAND NEEDS TO BE NEEDED

Did you know that men have a need to feel needed by their wives?

I (Connie) remember a discussion that my husband and I had once when he told me he felt I didn't need him. And I agreed completely. I was a product of my generation—I had come of age during the women's liberation movement, and although I was far from a women's libber I prided myself on being independent, self-sufficient, and able to take care of myself. I was *woman!* And I was part lion, too, for I sure could roar.

For the first several years of our marriage, Wes had a demanding schedule, and I had to take care of myself, and then later our twin daughters. There was no other choice. But now his schedule was more normal, and his remarks surprised me. I thought he would have preferred my independence, because it would seem his role then would be easier. But he didn't see it that way at all. He wanted to be needed.

I remember another time when I was sick for a few days and couldn't do much of anything. He even had to help me in and out of bed. I would have thought he would be thrilled to death when I was finally well, and he was, but the one thing I remember him saying after

I was back on my feet was how much he enjoyed my needing him during my illness.

It seems to us that a woman shouldn't have to become desperately sick in order for her husband to feel needed. Treating your husband as though he's not needed, believe it or not, undermines his sense of manhood.

Our husbands want to be our knights in shining armor, and they want us to see them that way as well. They want us to notice that they are knights! At the heart of who they are is their desire to love and protect us as wives. They want to be our lovers, defenders, providers, protectors, and "throw themselves in front of an oncoming train" kinds of men to us.

When a man feels unneeded, he has little motivation to talk. But when he begins to feel needed, he starts to see that you believe he brings something valuable and unique to the relationship. He sees that he meets a need in your life that no one else meets. He sees how you lean on him for strength and security. And he likes it.

You might try this. Share with your husband an area of your life in which he meets a need. Tell him what a wonderful job he does in meeting that need, and be specific. He may say very little, but we suspect he'll warm to the idea rather quickly, and you may well have unlocked a door that has been shut for perhaps a very long time.

Bottom Line: To say you no longer need the very one you once said you couldn't live without is sad indeed.

chapter twenty-three

SILENCE THE MARRIAGE SILENCER

How can marriage be so exhilarating and fulfilling one moment and then cold as Antarctica the next? How do you go from beautiful symphonies to playing off-key? What causes the "love noises" of a marriage to go silent? Why are so many marriages on life support? One of the primary reasons is lack of forgiveness.

If you ever had a gerbil, you certainly bought a cage. Part of the equipment was a water bottle that was inverted with a small aluminum tube projecting into his "kitchen," very near his food. Nearby was a wheel where the gerbil would spend hours running but never getting anywhere. This is a picture of what lack of forgiveness is like. One who does not forgive thinks she is moving forward in life, but she isn't and never will until she forgives. She just keeps going 'round and 'round, getting nowhere.

I (Nancy) recently had an encounter with a woman who was stuck in this cycle and didn't even know it. She was spinning her wheels, which were lubricated with tears. She shared that communication with her husband was almost nonexistent and that she was having a hard time even loving her nine-year-old son.

I asked her if she was holding back on forgiving anyone, and at first she appeared surprised by the question. As she mulled it over she continued to cry and revealed that she could not forgive someone for an egregious offense that had happened long ago.

She went on to say that as she thought about it, she really struggled in many relationships with members of her family. I explained how lack of forgiveness binds a person to offenses that have occurred in the past.[1] She told me that she had sought counsel from her pastor and that he told her that *she* couldn't forgive, but that she could ask Jesus to forgive the offender. This is simply not true. We are flooded with Scripture that tells *us* to forgive others as Jesus has forgiven us.[2]

I encouraged her to go home and settle this matter, asking God to forgive her for her lack of forgiveness, and urged her to forgive the person who had hurt her along with anyone else on her "list."

She did this. When I saw her a week later, she was positively radiant. She said she felt as though the weight of the world had been lifted from her shoulders. Not only had she forgiven the one who had so terribly hurt her; she was praying for him! No longer was she running and getting nowhere; she revealed that things were changing at home. She had a newfound love for her husband and son, and the lines of communication were now open. She had learned one of the most valuable lessons in life, which is that forgiveness brings healing and hope.

Bottom Line: Nothing kills communication faster than lack of forgiveness.

chapter twenty-four

CHOOSE TO FORGIVE

You can either master your feelings or allow them to master you. It's as simple as that.

Though women often think they have no choice but to live by their feelings, it is not true. You can choose to live otherwise. Frank B. Minirth and Paul D. Meier say that it's fine to try to understand our feelings as best we can, but the real focus shouldn't be on them—instead it should be on our behavior and our actions. They say, "In other words, your actions will determine how you feel."[1]

Forgiveness is not a feeling; it is a choice. You don't have to feel like forgiving someone in order to do so. You don't have to wait on him to change his ways, either. To do this puts *him* in control of *your* life. But by choosing to forgive him, you refuse to be imprisoned by the shackles of unforgivingness.

Jesus didn't allow His circumstances, His treatment from others, or His personal feelings get in the way of what His heavenly Father wanted Him to do. He wanted to follow God's will for His life, which included dying on a cross for our sins, so that we could live a life of freedom.

Forgiveness frees us to soar! Why choose to simply exist when you can live life to the max? Here are a few simple steps that will help you to do this:

1. **Pray fervently!** Ask God to forgive you for not extending forgiveness yourself. If you are holding something against your husband, ask God to help you to forgive him. Sometimes you can do this personally and privately before the Lord. Sometimes it may be necessary to graciously approach your husband and ask for his forgiveness. Be bold! Ask the Lord to orchestrate the time and place. Pray that your husband would have a receptive heart.
2. **Pursue reconciliation.** If the Lord impresses you to go to your husband, make certain that the kids will be elsewhere and that it will be just the two of you. One woman we know talked to her husband as they sat in the car in the garage after they had arrived home.
3. **Humbly confess your part.** Tell him that you know you have been unforgiving, and the result is that there are walls in your marriage. Refrain from mentioning how you feel he has contributed to these walls—let God be the one to convict him of that. What you are doing right now is asking forgiveness for your part in building the walls in your marriage, so make sure that is where the focus stays. Share with him that you have sought God's forgiveness, and now you are seeking his. This may feel awkward, but it is so worth it. Remember that God is right there with you.
4. **Use your free will** to make the choice to forgive.
5. **Deliberately behave** in a manner that the Lord has shown in the Bible to be right.
6. **Trust God** to do His part by renewing your mind and giving you new, transformed attitudes.[2]

We cannot stress strongly enough the powerful impact forgiveness will have on your marriage.

If you choose to do this, what might it look like? Perhaps something like this:

> "Joe, I don't know where to begin, so I'll just plunge right in. God has been convicting me lately about the walls I've put up in our marriage. I am so sorry I've done this. I've sought His forgiveness; now I'm asking you for yours. Will you forgive me?"

There's no way to know what your husband will say. Your humble apology may well be what causes your husband to consider what walls he may have built. He may even ask for your forgiveness in return. This, however, can't be your motive—to get your husband to fess up to what he's done. Your motive is to get your life lined up with God's Word, regardless of what your husband does or doesn't do. But notice that this is just a start! What's required of you from this point forward is to live a God-pleasing life, and that includes being willing to forgive your husband for future offenses that will occur.

Bottom Line: Forgiveness fans the flames of the burned-out hearth fires.

chapter twenty-five

KEEP THE PAST IN THE PAST

Real forgiveness is extravagant. Once you have forgiven, the past must remain in the past.

A friend of ours discovered this years ago. Her husband had engaged in an adulterous affair. She stayed with him, but only because of their young children. From her perspective all love was gone. He was extremely repentant and never strayed again. Over time a semblance of love and normalcy reentered their home. She felt she had "more or less" forgiven him.

However, one day she was talking to a friend about what it really means to forgive, and she realized she hadn't forgiven him at all.

> "It's as if I keep the memory of his affair in my hip pocket, and whenever it's to my advantage, I bring it out. I hold it over his head. I can do this without ever saying a word—I say plenty with my attitude and body language. I act as though he owes me for forgiving him and he'll never be able to pay off the debt. It's as if I'm letting him know that even when I stumble and fall in the marriage, nothing I ever do could possibly hurt him as much as he's hurt me. And he'd better not forget it.

What a terrible prison I've locked us both in. It's time for change."

And change she did. She went home, asked her husband's forgiveness, and purposed to live differently. An incredible peace enfolded their home that hadn't been there before. Her husband was finally released from the shackles of her unforgivingness, and she was released as well. Certainly we don't condone adultery—the Bible addresses it specifically and allows for grave consequences[1] because of it—but our point is to say that you can't forgive someone halfway. Either you forgive or you don't. There is no "you owe me" mentality left in the wake of forgiveness.

Forgiveness takes no hostages, and it doesn't quibble over piecemeal amounts. Forgive, and forgive completely. Don't dribble out little spoonfuls of forgiveness—be lavish with it! You'll be surprised to discover that when you do this you become the primary beneficiary of your own actions.

Go ahead, forgive your husband—over and over and over again. Do you think you can't do it because he doesn't deserve it? You don't forgive because another person deserves it or not. If that were the case, we'd all be doomed to spend eternity in hell. You forgive because God commands you to. You forgive to please Him.

Bottom Line: Forgiveness wipes the slate clean. If you live with past grievances, you will ruin your life.

chapter twenty-six

BE LOYAL

Success in marriage is more than finding the right person; it is becoming the right person. A vital ingredient in marriage is loyalty.

It has been said, *When the going gets tough, the tough get going.* But isn't it far harder to live out the reality of a more common scenario? Sometimes when the going gets tough, the weak cannot get going. That's when loyalty comes into play. *When the situation is difficult, the committed stand firm.*

There are legions of unsung heroes who stand by to protect the ones they love when everyone else wants to go the other way.

This very situation happened to our friend Sandy. Her husband had been put on life support following a stroke and a debilitating illness. He had signed a consent form to allow his removal from such a system should his condition warrant it. Sandy couldn't do it.

She had been told that she needed to let him go more times than she cared to count. He had lost the ability to speak. But there was something about the way he looked at her that kept her from making the decision he had agreed to earlier.

Sandy moved into her husband's room and rarely left his side. On an infrequent break she came to my office at the church. We prayed together in the sanctuary, prostrating ourselves before the Lord, beseeching Him to give her wisdom about this decision. We asked Him to heal John, as had hundreds of other faithful friends.

When she returned to the hospital, Sandy asked John if he wanted to live. He weakly nodded his head yes, and by the grace of God that was that. Sandy made a decision based on prayer and her husband's request. In the weeks that followed, John began to grow stronger. He spent more time off the respirator. Gradually he regained the capacity to breathe on his own with the help of a tracheotomy tube. Before long he was walking with the aid of a walker.

Shortly after that I saw him when he and Sandy came to our church. She poked her head in my office and asked if I would like to come out to the parking lot. She was running errands, she told me, and John was in the car!

I hurried out to see him. He was sitting in the front seat, smiling warmly at me. He still had the tracheotomy tube, and Sandy shared that he was being fed through a stomach tube and was also connected to a bag for his bladder. But he was alive! The tubes were to be removed in a few days.

Sandy was radiant as a litany of thanksgiving poured from John's lips. First he shared how grateful he was to God for His answer to the prayers of many. Then John looked at Sandy. He could barely express his appreciation for her devotion to him. He went on and on and on until his voice was reduced to a whisper.

What an impact her loyalty had on the many that knew them. John lived for several more months, and they both considered the extra time with each other the most precious they had shared as a couple.

Are you loyal? Can your husband count on you in the large as well as the everyday events that make up the bulk of your lives? Many a woman proclaims her loyalty, but who can find a trustworthy woman?[1]

Do you keep the personal things he tells you to yourself?

Do you refrain from talking about his faults to your parents, children, or friends?

Does your husband have full confidence in you?[2]

Can he entrust his reputation to you?

Is his name safe in your mouth?

Does your husband say, "You are never on my side"?

Do you subvert his parental authority, drawing the children to yourself, dismissing what their dad says?

Do you confess *his* sins to others?

Do you bring up his past mistakes?

Become loyal in the small, everyday things;[3] it is the training that prepares you for the times when the going gets tough.[4]

Bottom Line: Loyalty is a treasure that blesses both giver and recipient.

chapter twenty-seven

BECOME HIS CHEERLEADER

One of the wisest things you can do when your husband is experiencing storms is to be his cheerleader. When everything else is swirling around him, he needs to know that your faith in him remains stronger than ever.

A storm that hit my (Nancy) husband's life years ago is one of the more debilitating ones that a man will ever face: job loss.

"I just called to tell you I no longer have a job," Ray said over the phone.

"Don't kid around like that," I replied. "It's not funny!"

"I'm not kidding," he said. "The company is downsizing. Don't you remember my telling you about it? Now my position has been declared *no longer necessary*. I'll be home in thirty minutes."

My heart was heavy, not only for Ray but for my entire family. My nest had been touched, and my feeling of security was gone. A few minutes later, I saw his car pull into the driveway. Ray got out of the car with the saddest expression I'd ever seen on his face. He opened the rear door and fumbled around to retrieve something from the backseat. It was a cardboard box, not very large, but big enough to hold the contents of his desk. Other boxes in the backseat containing the paraphernalia from his office would be brought in later.

He walked in the door, put the box on the kitchen table—it represented a large part of his life for the past twenty years—and slumped into a chair. For the first time in our many years together he cried. People had long referred to him as the golden boy. He was the vice president and was being groomed as the next president of the company. But companies have a way of being sold; new presidents are "enthroned," and golden boys become extra baggage that the new team doesn't want.

How does a woman live with a husband who is depressed, angry, wounded, distressed, remote, and uncommunicative? How does she have conversations with a man who has been traumatized and really doesn't care about anything but his own grief?

There are practical things as well as spiritual things you can do when your husband is heartbroken over some of life's biggest storms.

1. Take the matter to God in prayer.[1] Perhaps your prayer life is an up-and-down struggle, as mine was when Ray lost his job. Realize that God has your life in His hands. You belong to Him—you are His child—and therefore you are His responsibility. Commit this situation to Him, and ask Him to help you be a supportive wife. Ask God to keep you free of anxiety[2] and enable you to be a helper[3] to your husband.

One woman recalled that she did not handle this very same situation well. She sorrowfully related that when this happened to her husband she responded in a verbally abusive way. Her fear overcame her, and she angrily told him what she thought of a man who couldn't keep a job. This not only pushed her husband further away, but also put him into such a state of depression that he could barely function.

2. Be a woman of the Word.[4] Get into the Bible for personal comfort and to see what God says about your behavior and conversation. One of the things that His Word says over and over is that we should *love one another as He has loved us.*[5] There will be days when your husband takes his bitterness out on you, and days when he is completely unlovable. Remember your vow to love him for better *and* for worse, for richer *and* for poorer. What does it say about the shallowness of your own character if you only love your husband when the skies are blue and the storms are far, far away?

When you choose to live in a godly way, you bring glory to God, and you grow in character as well. Stormy weather is a wonderful opportunity to pour out love on your stricken husband—verbally as well as physically.

3. Become your husband's cheerleader. Have you noticed that cheerleaders never seem to give up? Whether their team is ahead or behind, one thing is certain: They are behind the team! *Two, four, six, eight, who do we appreciate?* They call out the name of the team or of a particular player. *You can do it; you can do it, if you put your mind to it!*

Professional sports players often attribute a close win to the cheering fans—saying that their support is what provided the extra momentum to win the game. Are you your husband's cheerleader? Can he count on you for support? The situation in your husband's life is an opportunity to lay aside your personal comfort and begin investing heavily in your husband's stock. He may continue to mourn week after week, and there may seem to be no return on your investment. But don't give up!

One woman we know thought up various cheers to lift her husband's bleak spirit. One day a particular phrase grabbed his attention. She said, in her best cheerleader voice, "*They may have knocked you down, but they can never knock you out!* With God's help, you have overcome greater adversity than this. I believe in you!" It was as though her husband woke up.

He repeated the phrase over and over again. "You're right! They can knock me down, but they can't knock me out!" It was through her unwavering, loving behavior that communication opened up between them once again. He trusted her love for him and began to confide in her more deeply and intimately than ever before. He began sending out resumes; as he waited to hear back, he took a part-time job at a hardware store to occupy his time and pad his checking account. It wasn't long before their prayers were answered and he found a job that was just right for him.

The same thing happened to my (Nancy) husband, Ray. He got a call from a company in North Carolina and became president of a company there. Not too long after that he also became a Christian.

4. Keep on keeping on no matter what. One wife we know is married to a man who has been depressed by the personal tragedy of a sudden death. This depression has been going on for several years. Nothing seems able to bring him out of it. He will have a few good days, and then once again be enveloped by grief. He's seldom in a good mood and has difficulty sleeping and concentrating. His conversation repeatedly returns to the subject of his sorrow. Something that adds to the problem is that he won't seek outside help.

What many women would do is finally declare, "I have had it!" "You have to get over this!" or "Get some help or I am leaving!" But our friend has chosen to stay by his side. She was there when the going was good, and now that the going is tough she is committed to seeing her husband through this difficulty. In her case her husband wants to talk things over and even though she has heard it before, she has chosen to be his sounding board. She is growing in her faith and in her character. This is not the way she would have chosen to grow, but she is bowing to the sovereignty of God and clinging to Him for help. You can as well![6]

5. If necessary, get help yourself. You might need to go to your pastor, a trustworthy Christian counselor, or a godly older woman who would consider mentoring you.

Bottom Line: Cheer your husband on when the going gets tough.

part three

About You

I didn't know that!

It's fun being a girl.
We can experiment with lipstick and wear cute clothes.
We can buy shoes that don't fit just because they're on sale.
We can order from a menu and then change our minds.
Six times.
We can laugh one minute and cry the next.
And we can feel lots better simply by being hugged
and eating a piece of chocolate.

Who am I, anyway? Haven't you asked that question about yourself from time to time ever since you were a little girl? Do you remember this nursery rhyme: "What are little girls made of? …Sugar and spice and everything nice, that's what little girls are made of"? Maybe you liked that rhyme. Or maybe you thought little boys sounded like a lot more fun— "…Snippets and snails and puppy dog tails, that's what little boys are made of."

It's an age-old question, and we invite you to look at it again. As we have visited, worked with, and taught hundreds of women during the past twenty years, we know our subject well. We have learned the hard way much of what you will be reading in the next section. We address some subjects that aren't often talked about. *What do I do with these hormones? How can I avoid bitterness? Can I develop thicker skin? What if he doesn't meet my needs? What can I do to reinvigorate the intimacy we shared when we were first married?* And of course, *Why doesn't he talk to me?*

As you take this information into account, one of the first things you may notice is your husband's newfound interest in you. Talking with you is no longer threatening or scary; it is fun. Laughter and private jokes become the norm. We know one husband who stated publicly and with unabashed tears before a large group, "I cannot begin to express the effect that her transformation has had on me and our family." His wife was nearby, in tears as well.

Let's take the lid off the box! You are a woman; you are a daughter, sister, friend, and possibly a mother. You work, for all women are working women. You are busy, but certainly not too busy to develop a sensational relationship with your husband.

chapter twenty-eight

TEND THE GARDEN

Not long ago we heard an interview with Dr. Kevin Leman, a bestselling author and speaker. Dr. Leman suggested that if a woman wanted to get her husband's attention (and he's far more likely to talk if she has his attention), one of the best things she could do was slip a personal article of her clothing into his briefcase along with a little note. He said if she *really* wanted to get his attention, the note might say something like, *The kids will be at Grandma's tonight. Can't wait for you to come home.*

I (Connie) was telling my husband about this, and he thought this was absolutely brilliant. I think he was ready to nominate Dr. Leman for the Nobel Peace Prize.

The next day I was working at my computer and the phone rang. It was my husband.

"I'm still looking," he said.

"For what?" I asked.

"You know..." he said.

"No, I don't," I responded. "What are you talking about?"

"I'm searching in my briefcase for something in particular, and it's not there!"

"Oh!" Now I got it, and, no, it wasn't there. "Scientific study has proven that intermittent reinforcement is the most effective," I replied, joining the game. "Keep looking. Maybe one of these days you'll find something."

"What if I have a heart attack first?" he asked. "You'd better make it sooner than later."

The reality is that my husband probably *would* have a heart attack if he ever found something like that in his briefcase—because he wouldn't think it was mine! That's how staid and stodgy I had become over time. What a legacy: *She was a good, staid, stodgy, predictable woman*. It was time for a change!

The moral of this story is that you should be careful what you tell your husband. Seriously, though, sex is extremely important to a man, and he prefers captivating and intriguing over staid and stodgy. In his same talk, Dr. Leman cited a study that had been done where men and women were asked to rank what they enjoyed doing most in their spare time. Not surprisingly, sex ranked number one for men; but for women it ranked number fourteen—right after gardening! This led him to conclude that sex begins in the garden—which it did, the Garden of Eden. But that's another topic.

Meeting your husband's sexual needs is one of the most effective things you can do to begin to get him to talk to you, *for if he's feeling thwarted or frustrated sexually, he is not going to be chatty.* That may be the biggest understatement in this book.

Often women make the mistake of withholding sex and using it as leverage to make husbands change in certain areas. This causes more problems than it solves. Although she may get what she wants, it will come at a high price. Her husband will begin to resent both her and her controlling, manipulative ways.

If you want communication with your husband to increase (and more importantly, if you want to honor God with your life), don't use his natural, God-given desire for sex against him in this way. He knows what you're doing and loathes it. Holding out until you get your way undermines your husband's masculinity and chips away at the very essence of who he was created to be.

Do you recognize yourself in any of these areas?

1. **Finances.** Don't insist he either go along with a purchase—big or small—or "suffer the consequences." Don't buy, or ask him to buy, what you can't afford or don't need—clothes, furniture, jewelry, cars, houses, vacations, etc. Don't sneak purchases into the house and then reward him with intimacy to assuage your own conscience.
2. **Household chores.** Do you have the mind-set that once he starts helping around the house you will consider his sexual advances? You may need to ask him to help you, but don't punish him by withholding sex if he doesn't do his part around the house or doesn't do it to your satisfaction.
3. **Social Functions.** Perhaps you are more social than he is. Don't promise him a night he'll never forget if he'll accompany you to certain parties or places. Give him nights he won't forget without a price tag attached. He may or may not become more social, but sex shouldn't be used to force him to become someone he isn't. We know of one woman who became so upset with her husband for not regularly attending their Sunday school class that she revoked his right to her body.[1]
4. **Raising the children.** If his method of child rearing is different than yours, talk about it. If you have valid concerns, talk to a pastor or counselor. But don't use sex as a way of gaining the upper hand.

Generally a woman's ability to share joyfully in the sexual act hinges on one thing: whether or not she feels loved by her husband. If she doesn't, she is not likely to be overly enthusiastic when it comes to the sexual relationship. This is an especially tricky area. A husband may be unaware of the need she has to feel loved because he perceives love so differently. Sex to a woman is far more about romance than the act itself. To a man, it's often more about the act and the pleasure that accompanies it. Yes, it gets complicated.

If your husband gets up, goes to work, and brings home a paycheck, chances are he's assuming that you are feeling loved because that's one of the major ways men show love. So while you are waiting, he's thinking he's already given what you're waiting for.

So don't just tell him you need to feel loved. Help your man out. Be specific and tell him what kinds of things would make you feel that way. For instance:

- "You know, darling, I would love it if you held me at times other than when you wanted sex." This may sound too direct, but remember that men like direct! They are goal oriented, and your directions facilitate their achieving the goal.
- "I love it when you call me from work—it makes me feel so special."
- "It feels so good when you hold my hand while we're walking."
- "It is so romantic when you take time to listen to my point of view on things."
- "What do I want for my birthday? I'd love it if you brought me a single red rose—that would make me feel so loved." Help him remember special dates like this ahead of time. Don't set him up for failure. Some women make these dates a "love test" that their husbands fail.
- "Your helping bathe the kids at night makes me feel nurtured."
- "When you put your arms around me and ask about my day before you read the newspaper, it says you're more concerned about me than you are about last night's football game."
- "I love it when you rub my shoulders...scratch my back...massage my feet...."

Bottom Line: Your husband needs to feel that he's a wonderful lover. Make him feel like Romeo whenever you can.

chapter twenty-nine

COME-ONS—EIGHTEEN TIPS YOUR HUSBAND WILL LOVE

Are sexually fulfilled husbands more talkative? One would certainly wonder if the two don't go together.

We asked a class of eighty women this question, and 90 percent of them felt that their husbands were more communicative when their sexual needs were met. The other 10 percent were too shocked to answer either way! We had a pastor ask a large group of men this same question, and virtually every hand was raised. Some men probably raised both hands! It seems to us that sexual fulfillment and good communication often go hand in hand.

Maybe you need a shot in the arm in this area. Maybe you've become rather lackadaisical about it, don't give it much thought. Maybe you're thinking that once your husband starts talking to you you'll become more interested in meeting his sexual needs.

Here's a challenge for you: Why not take some action anyway? While you're mulling that possibility, here are some tips to get you started.

1. Talk about your relationship during nonheated times and in a neutral place. Agree ahead of time that you will be open and honest. Guard against offending or being offended.
2. If you need counsel, seek it.
3. Leave notes for him saying how much you love him.
4. Call him during the day—leave a voice mail on his answering machine.
5. Send him a card. This can touch a man far more than you realize. We know of a pastor who says he wouldn't be married today if it weren't for a card he received thirty-three years ago and has kept!
6. Tell him something he does that makes you feel special or loved.
7. Laugh at an old memory.
8. Reminisce about how far you've come.
9. Appreciate his strengths, and tell him what those are.
10. Do something spontaneous.
11. If you have young children who don't sleep through the night, ask a friend or family member to take them for a few hours while you and your husband have a date.
12. Be creative! One woman we know sent her husband on a scavenger hunt, much to his delight.
13. Plan a special outing for your husband—make it something he enjoys.
14. Reserve a hotel room...camp in the backyard...sleep in front of the fireplace.
15. Make yourself available, and let him know that you are.
16. Be interested...be playful...replace the "spark plugs," so to speak.
17. Create atmosphere—soft music, candlelight, a warm bath, etc. These kinds of things lend themselves to romance.
18. Shave your legs. There's something about smooth legs that makes a woman feel sexy.

Bottom Line: Fireworks are not only for the Fourth of July.

chapter thirty

REFRESH YOUR LOVEMAKING

Here are eighteen more tips we think your husband will love.

1. Take a brief rest or short nap, so you're not so tired at night. Research shows that naps beyond forty minutes cause you to wake up feeling groggy because they give your body time to enter deep sleep.
2. If you work outside the home, try driving home with relaxing music playing in the background or without the radio at all. A quiet, peaceful drive can be refreshing.
3. Don't speak of your husband's sexual performance to others—whether glowingly or not so glowingly. His sexual performance shouldn't be fodder for your casual conversations with friends and family members. Your friends may laugh, but remember that they're laughing at the expense of your husband. Be 100 percent loyal to him in this area.
4. Rent an old black-and-white love story, and watch it by candlelight.

5. Be explicit in letting your husband know what you enjoy: "I like it when you do such and such." Men love these kinds of directions. It's affirming for a man to know that you think he's a great lover. What if he's not? Help him become one. Your affirmation and acceptance are what will make this happen. As the years go by in your marriage you will become more and more familiar with your own personal "map." Become a good topographer, and suggest fun places to visit and those worth lingering over.
6. Be the one to begin to break down the walls in this area. Maybe things have become a bit boring and predictable. Become Mrs. Unpredictable.
7. Let him know when you're feeling especially sensuous. We have a good friend who hung a blue garter casually on the bedpost when this was the case for her. Her husband soon discovered a love for blue garters that he'd never known before.
8. Ask him what he likes. Then consider doing it. Be the initiator! This man is your husband, and you were created to enjoy each other's bodies.
9. Plan a treasure hunt for your husband. The first note might tell him to look in the kitchen, where he would find a second, which would lead him to the third, and so on. The last note would lead him to you—the treasure. It could be that he would find you in a place in your home that you've never reserved for such a "party."
10. Save money for an overnight stay at a bed-and-breakfast. If your husband isn't a B&B man (one of ours isn't), book a suite at a local hotel. Many of the economy chains have suites for moderate prices. It sparks conversation when the children are not the focal point of the evening and he is.
11. Place a warm call to his workplace (if the line is private) and invite him to a "date evening" at home.
12. Begin wearing the kind of nightwear he stopped giving you because you were always cold.

13. Start talking during intimacy, and tell him what he means to you and what you are experiencing. He'll deeply appreciate your participation and praise.
14. Smile suggestively when he broaches the subject of togetherness early on in the evening. Make lots of eye contact with an "I can't wait until the kids are in bed" look.
15. Reintroduce the "eyeing his body" gaze, and then look into his eyes. Even if his body is not like a movie star's, it should be a source of wonder to you.
16. Remind yourself what a privilege it is to be married. Many women long for a husband. You've got one! Thank God for him.
17. Drop in on him in the shower and whistle appreciatively.
18. Give him a lingering kiss. Not a peck, but one that's meaningful and conveys your appreciation of him as a man.

Bottom Line: Take him on a memorable trip tonight. And tomorrow night, too.

chapter thirty-one

HOUSEKEEPING

There are a few housekeeping matters regarding sex that are worth mentioning.

Avoid putting yourself in the position of rejecting your husband's sexual advances. If you are not feeling well, or if there are other circumstances that will keep you from intimacy, simply let him know up front. Don't allow him to risk being amorous if you know he has no chance of success. This is humiliating and should be a rare event. It may lead to temptation as well.[1] If this occurs frequently, his sexual interest will likely decrease, and his frustration and resentment toward you will increase. Soon he may stop initiating at all and become distant, cold, and sometimes even harsh.

A friend of ours, who spends many of her days chasing after young children, is often mentally and physically exhausted by bedtime. Yet she wants to meet her husband's sexual needs. "This might not be the 'full bells and whistles extravaganza,'" she tells him. "It might just be a simple rendition of it. We'll see." In this way she lets her husband know she is still willing, although she might not be as passionate and energized as she normally is.

If you're exhausted and Mr. Ever Ready is about to explode, ask the Lord to energize you. One of the godliest women we know did this when her children were young, and now, thirty years later, she says she cherishes greatly the sexual intimacy she continues to share with her husband.

Finally, a man doesn't want his wife to simply "endure" the sexual encounter out of obligation or duty. He hopes for her mutual participation, satisfaction, and enjoyment. Although a one-sided sexual encounter meets his desire for sexual release, it can create a void and emptiness that leaves him questioning his ability as a man. There is something about a man's self-concept that is mysteriously tied to his sexual performance. Affirm your husband in his role as lover. He'll appreciate it far more than you realize.

Some might think that until communication is improved in a marriage, the sexual relationship can't be improved. This simply isn't true. Your efforts to meet your husband's needs in this area could well be what will reestablish the line of communication between you.

Bottom Line: Be a great housekeeper.

chapter thirty-two

GET A GRIP ON YOUR HORMONES

Sometimes it's nothing more than those infamous monthly hormones that can keep your husband from wanting to get near you, let alone talk to you.

In the delightful and poignant book *Emotional Phases of a Woman's Life,* British author Jean Lush talks about the pressures she experienced as her well-intentioned mother tried to mold her into a proper young woman.

> I thought that...I was not allowed to feel the negative emotions that almost overwhelmed me on those days before my period. That was another thing: One never talked about *that.* If you *had* to discuss it, you would whisper, "I'm coming on unwell."
>
> I grew up thinking it was all right to swoon or to have a bad head, but never, never, never were we to discuss our bodies or what was happening to them. I remember one day mentioning the word brassiere to my father. Let me tell you, Mother went white. She rolled her eyes and gave me that tight-lipped look, as only Mother could.

...I eventually got married, and to my utter shock a few months after our wedding, my very understanding husband said to me, "I'm not going to listen to you today." (We were having an argument about money or some such thing.) "We'll talk about it after your period, when you're back to your old self."

I couldn't believe that he would mention *it,* but I was so thankful. I'd never really related my days of being an absolute monster to my "coming on unwell."[1]

Your husband has probably noticed when you're "coming on unwell," and no doubt he doesn't understand all that goes along with it. Let's journey through a typical month to see how hormones might affect a woman.

Week 1: This begins on the first day of a woman's period. Her energy is high, and there is nothing she can't do. She rises early, has a fabulous quiet time with the Lord, and makes out a to-do list for the rest of the year. Today she plans on cleaning not just the house, but the attic and basement as well—all by noon. She gets so much done that she amazes even herself.

She loves their little house. Though it's small, it reminds her of a warm English cottage, and she wouldn't trade it for the world. She may even crochet some lace valances for the living-room windows. Wouldn't it be fun to see them blowing in the breeze?

Her children are angels, and her husband is Mr. Wonderful. She whips up a seven-course meal for supper, and her family is delighted. Life is great. She wouldn't change a thing. She stays up until midnight planning all she'll get done the next day—by noon.

Week 2: Still brimming with lots of energy, she narrows her focus down to specific activities instead of "going all out." She has her quiet time and then plans her day, pacing herself a little more than before. Her to-do list is more realistic; she plans to get the bathrooms cleaned and the laundry done by noon.

She makes time to sit out on the front porch and enjoy the sun's warm rays. She takes time to smell the flowers. She finds herself dreaming of the days ahead. She feels calm and serene and worries very little.

She decides to make sheers for the windows instead of crocheting lace valances. It won't take as much time, but they'll still look charming.

The children remain angelic, and Mr. Wonderful still slips in to bed beside her each night. She whips up a four-course meal for supper, and life continues on its pleasant path. *I am such a fortunate woman,* she thinks.

Week 3: Her energy level has receded, and much of her enthusiasm for life is gone. She rushes through her quiet time and doesn't get as much out of it as before. It seems she can't get anything done around the house. What took her ten minutes to do two weeks ago now seems to take hours.

Johnny spilled jelly on her freshly mopped floor, and for some reason she feels like sobbing about it. She feels irritated that he didn't pick up the jar with both hands like she'd taught him. She begins to doubt herself and her abilities. What kind of mother can't teach her child how to pick up a jar of jelly?

The windows remain bare. Why did she think she could sew valances? She hates sewing, and the end product always looks like it's homemade anyway. Her little English cottage seems dark, dank, and crowded. *It will take more than valances to brighten up this place,* she thinks as a sense of sadness seeps in.

She feels tired and would like nothing more than to take a nap. The children are getting on her nerves—they seem so needy all of a sudden. She wishes Mr. Wonderful would take a course in Minor Home Repairs. But he'd probably fail it. The blahs have hit and hit hard. Nothing seems to be going right.

For supper she fixes a casserole and opens a can of fruit. She can't wait until the kids are in bed so she can take a bath and go to bed.

Week 4: This is the week prior to menstruation. Tension mounts and she finds herself more and more agitated. She has one nerve left, and her husband and children seem intent on jumping up and down on it. The only time she's not snapping at them is when they're at school and work. Her head is throbbing and the day drags on endlessly. She can't seem to work up the energy to get anything done. Her quiet time seems dry and takes so much effort. She feels like she weighs five hundred pounds. Nothing looks good on her—not even her favorite outfit.

She is exhausted and wants to withdraw from life. Even her closest friends get on her nerves. She looks around her house and wonders when they will be able to afford a larger home. This place is slowly driving her insane.

She fixes grilled cheese sandwiches for the third night in a row and says that if anyone grumbles, they can fix their own supper. She goes to bed early. Life seems so difficult.

A few days later her period begins. She wakes up with a renewed sense of energy and purpose, and the cycle begins anew. She's back to wanting to clean the house, stencil the hallway, and wallpaper the kitchen all in two hours. Life is so wonderful.

The roller coaster of hormones! What can you do about them? We suggest the following:

- Familiarize yourself with your cycle.
- Know when to expect the low times, and prepare for them.
- Be vigilant in guarding your words and your actions when your hormones rage.
- Make maximum use of your "up" times—sort of like the ant preparing for winter.
- Don't put too many demands on yourself during the low times.
- Get plenty of rest.
- Freeze a few meals to have on hand when you don't feel like cooking.
- Remember that the difficult times will soon pass.

- Eat healthy foods, and resist the urge to binge on chocolate or junk food.
- If the low times seem to hang around far too long, seek medical intervention.
- Spend time with God every day, even when you don't feel like it. Just a few minutes with Him can strengthen you.

We've had women tell us that a daily dose of vitamin B6 works wonders for them when they experience menstrual difficulties. Some say just an aspirin or two helps alleviate their discomfort. There are many products available; perhaps one would be of benefit to you.

When Jean Lush addressed the subject of hormonal activity and women's emotions on *Focus on the Family,* the show received the largest response ever.[2] Certainly hormones are an issue for women in America, and you will do yourself a favor to learn about them and how they affect your life and your marriage. We highly recommend *Emotional Phases of a Woman's Life* to learn more about your monthly cycle and all it entails. Covering the gamut of hormones from A to Z, this book also discusses menopause in depth and the many changes that accompany it.

Bottom Line: When your hormones take you on a roller coaster, go along with the ride.

chapter thirty-three

YOUR UNHAPPINESS AFFECTS YOUR MATE

Did you know that when you're unhappy your husband feels responsible? He does. Whether it has anything to do with him or not, he feels that it is part of his role as a husband to assure that you are happy. And when you're not, he feels that he has failed in that role.

Many women don't realize this because they don't feel the same way. If a woman's husband is unhappy, she doesn't take it personally or feel it is her fault. Men internalize their spouses' unhappiness while women do not. When you are feeling unhappy, the best thing you can say to your husband is, "This has absolutely nothing to do with you." Saying this to your husband when you're feeling blue prevents him from personalizing your unhappiness. We can't overemphasize how important this is to do.

A friend called me (Connie) the other night and told me she felt sad. A number of things were going on with her children and with her work as well, causing her to be irritable and upset. I asked how her husband was handling this. She said, "He's gone into his own little quiet zone."

I asked if she realized that when she was unhappy her husband took it personally. She had never heard of such a thing. So I encouraged her to ask him about it. She did and was surprised to discover that it was true. He told her, "When you're unhappy, I feel responsible—like I'm not doing something I'm supposed to."

When you are unhappy, your husband probably won't feel compelled to coax out of you what is wrong. Instead he will probably become quiet and wait on you to get over it. Men are problem solvers, but our sadness is one problem they don't quite know what to do with.

You can help your husband immensely in this area by asking God to give you a spirit of contentment then refusing to be a martyr. It is a taxing thing to live with a woman who is chronically unhappy or disgruntled. Nothing weighs a man down quite so much as a complaining spirit. If he's weighted down, he will most likely withdraw.

Likewise, deep sighs indicating that you wish your life were different are really not a fair burden to put on a man. He may wish his life were different, too, yet he continues on. Can you imagine how wearying it would be if he were the one who sighed heavily?

"A cheerful heart is good medicine, but a crushed spirit dries up the bones."[1] It seems to us that many people are too busy these days. Try to make time to be cheerful. Think afresh of all God has done in your life and look anew at your husband. Give him a gift that he will value highly and that will set him free as well: the gift of a cheerful, positive wife.

Bottom Line: Don't dry up your husband's bones.

chapter thirty-four

WHAT DO I DO WITH THESE FEELINGS?

"Well then," you might be asking, "if I want my husband to talk to me, can I ever tell him how I'm feeling, or do I have to learn to 'stuff' everything?"

Of course you can tell him how you're feeling. Stuffing your emotions is just as unhealthy as being overly dramatic and hysterical. The real caveat, though, is learning how to share with him how you're feeling without making him feel attacked and responsible.

First, take time to figure out what it is that's really bothering you, for often feelings and emotions cloud the real issue. Second, choose a time to talk to him about it when you won't be distracted, interrupted, or pressed for time. If you have to ask a friend to watch your kids for an hour or so, or hire a baby-sitter, do it. It will be money well spent.

Not long ago, my (Connie) family and I were visiting my parents. My father feels strongly that a man should remove his cap or hat at mealtime. This is how he was brought up, and it is a big deal to him.

My husband was brought up this way as well, and nearly always does unless he's been playing golf all afternoon and has "cap hair"—hair that's been smashed down for four or five hours under a cap.

When this happens, he feels his disheveled, smashed hair is far worse to look at than a cap.

On this occasion, he and my three brothers-in-law had been golfing all afternoon. They came in just in time to join us for sandwiches. I noticed that Wes left his cap on.

"Would you mind taking your cap off?" I asked him.

Before I could say anything else, everyone had gathered around, and we began eating. His cap was still on. His actions greatly upset me, and I wanted to let him know that they did.

However, I knew from years of past experience that the best time to talk isn't at the height of anger. So I seethed my way through the meal and tried to ignore his cap, which now seemed to be shining like a beacon to me. I was certain it was to everyone else, too.

It's amazing how twenty-four hours can put a different skew on things. I actually gave myself three days to mull over what had happened and what the issue was really all about. I found that the real issue wasn't whether or not Wes wore a cap at the table (although that was still an issue) but whether he cared about my feelings and whether he realized he had shown disrespect to my dad.

When I finally approached him, I was calm and coherent. Had I approached him earlier, I would have immediately placed him on the defensive with my barrage of words and emotions and never gotten to the real point. I told him how his actions had made me feel and that I felt he'd shown disrespect to my dad.

Doing this not only gave me Wes's full attention, but it also allowed him to listen without feeling he had to defend himself at every turn. Often you are the tone setter in these kinds of situations. If you attack and blame, he'll counterattack and blame as well. But if you are calm and respectful, most likely he will be, too. In this case, my calmness (which can't be a front for hidden anger, by the way) let him see that my intention wasn't to accuse or condemn, but simply to let him know how his actions made me feel.

What was the outcome? He felt terrible that he'd not removed his cap. He said that of course he would never intentionally hurt my father or me. He remembered me asking him to take it off, but in the craziness of so much going on and so many people around he'd simply forgotten to.

Ironically, I was talking to my mother a few weeks afterward, and neither she nor my father had noticed Wes's cap. It was a far bigger deal to me than it was to my dad.

You can help your guy learn to understand "gal" by remembering that he doesn't understand how your minds works (who has ever understood how a woman's mind works?). Reminding him of a few basic things that are common to women may help him better understand:

1. If you perceive that I'm upset, I most likely am. Ask me more than once if there's anything going on. I know this sounds strange to you, but sometimes I won't automatically say what's bothering me unless I feel like you're interested enough to pursue it.
2. Don't try to solve my problems when I'm upset. Just be there for me and listen. That's the best thing you can do.
3. Assure me that you love me. Hold my hand. Look at me. Whatever is going on, these kinds of things will make it better.
4. If I continue to withdraw or act weird, don't take it personally.
5. Say, "I want to help, but I don't know what to do. What can I do that would help you the most?" If I say, "Nothing," offer to help again later.

These tips won't cause him to understand you completely, but they will go a long way.

Bottom Line: Honey is sweeter than lemons. If you have that "heads are gonna roll" feeling when getting ready to talk to your husband about something that bothers you, don't say a word!

chapter thirty-five

RECOGNIZE FAMILIAL PATTER

An evening can be ruined by the oddest things if you let it—such as an honest remark by a man who really loves you but who expresses himself in a way that may be unfamiliar to you and your family.

Each family of origin has developed its own patter, its own specialized lingo, which often seems to a new bride (or an old bride!) the only correct and socially acceptable dialect on earth. And pity the unsuspecting bridegroom who discovers he has married a woman who is easily offended by comments his birth family considers the norm.

We will tell you from the vantage point of studying this phenomenon for years: Your husband will not lose his gift of familial patter!

It was early on in my (Nancy) marriage when I began to notice this. The way Ray expressed himself became an issue with me. This began to trouble him, and the memory of his heartfelt admission lingers to this day: "I just don't know how to talk to you!"

He was right. I remember wondering why it was that he couldn't talk to me the way my dad, mom, and sister did.

In fact, to this day my sister and I speak something of a foreign language when we get together. I think Dad taught us this! I'm not sure how we learned it or when we discovered we had this sublanguage capability. But I don't think we are the only family of origin with a communication style that is lost on those who join the family by marriage.

Allow me to illustrate. When I go to visit my sister Christine in Dallas, she makes a huge production of welcoming me. My room is lovingly prepared with fresh flowers. She has a gift for me. She pampers me like visiting royalty—I must admit that I like this sort of treatment. I do the same for her when she visits. It isn't too long into these visits that we lapse, without thinking, into *sistertalk*.

For instance if I say, "Isn't it cozy in here?" she looks aghast. She'll exclaim, "You're hot! Darling, why didn't you tell me? I'm so sorry; let me turn on the air!"

If she says, "Do you want to go to the IMAX Theater? They are having a wonderful show that simulates climbing Mount Everest."

All I have to say is, "That sounds interesting and a bit exciting."

She will exclaim, "What was I thinking? You're afraid of heights—of course we won't go there! I had forgotten that the last time we went and saw the helicopter ride over the Grand Canyon you wrapped both arms around the supporting post in the theater!" (This is a true story.)

My sister and I have interchanges like this often. Sometimes she initiates sistertalk and sometimes I do. Now how hard would this be for Ray to learn? It makes me smile to think of it. I have given him sistertalk lessons for *years*, and he is simply not interested.

I remember asking Ray one beautiful, sunny day, "When you were a little boy, did you ever lie down on the grass, look up at the shape of the clouds, and think, *That looks like a cat, or that resembles a boat floating on a calm blue sea*"?

He said, "No, we were too busy working on our ranch just trying to survive from one day to the next. If I were lying on the ground, it would have been to look up a tree to find a squirrel or raccoon for my mother to cook for dinner!"

I remember thinking, *What a killjoy!* But actually he was simply responding truthfully.

Why don't we just say what we think? And why don't we freely accept what our husbands say and the way they package it? It is no understatement when we tell you this is a hot issue for a man.

How are you doing in this area?

Bottom Line: If you want a deafening silence in your marriage, insist that your husband respond like you.

chapter thirty-six

DON'T PLAY THE SEMANTICS GAME

Because women are more verbal than men, one of the things they often get caught up in is what we call the semantics game. We could go into how the game is played, but we suspect most women will know what we're talking about.

For example, every Sunday after church, Joe says, "How about going to the Chicken Wing and grabbing some lunch?"

Since Joe says this in the form of a question, Mary figures she has every right to say either yes or no or to suggest something else. Technically she's right. But here's the deal: She's been married to Joe for twenty years, and she knows that what he's really saying is, "I've thought through where I'd like to go, and this is it." Yet it annoys her that he won't say what he really means: "I'd like to go to the Chicken Wing."

She says, "If he wants to go there, then that's what he should say. He should leave out 'how about.' As long as he phrases it the way he does, though, I'll never say, 'Great idea.' I'll keep adding my two cents about other restaurants."

She proceeds to pick a fight, saying she's not in the mood for chicken and would prefer tacos, even though she says it rarely matters to her. But she's determined to break him of the irritating way he phrases things. So with bulldog tenacity she advances quickly around the semantic game board.

Mary often wonders why her husband doesn't talk to her much. Hmm...any ideas?

No man enjoys having his English dissected, diagrammed, and picked apart. He doesn't want every detail that flows from his mouth to be corrected. He feels like he's a walking report card, and he doesn't like it. Nor does he like verbal tag or playing this weird game that his wife seems to enjoy so much.

We speak from experience. We are both former champions of this game. You may prove your point and even get him to agree that you're technically correct, but so what? Are you really getting what you want?

If you know what he's really trying to say, accept it as just that. Stop insisting he "get it right" before you engage in communication with him. Become his advocate.

Begin listening to him with fresh ears! Listen to how he says things, and hear what he's trying to say. This increases the value of your stock as well as encourages him to talk.

Bottom line: Throw away the semantics game board.

chapter thirty-seven

CONTROL THE URGE TO CONTROL

Has the song "Anything You Can Do, I Can Do Better" become the theme of your marriage?

Control has been an issue with which women have wrestled ever since time began.[1] Many women tell us that they don't struggle with issues of control—as long as their husbands are doing what they want them to do!

A wonderful way to begin rebuilding your relationship with your husband is to let go of the control within your home. This is a simple concept that seems difficult to put into practice. We like things done the way we like things done, right?

My (Connie) husband used to say that the moment we drove into our driveway I became a different person. My normally laid-back personality flew the coop, and my commander-in-charge personality moved in. Wes really disliked this. I had a certain way I wanted things done and, in my mind at least, they were far superior to his.

When he helped dress the girls, I couldn't understand why he'd pair a pink shirt with green pants.

If he helped in the kitchen, I expected him to wipe up any spills—the moment they were spilled. "You don't even let it hit the ground before you're telling me to wipe it up," he would say.

When he took a shower, I didn't think there should be any wet towels hanging anywhere but over the towel rack, and they shouldn't be folded in two because they took too long to dry that way.

The address book should always be put away; balled up socks were not acceptable in the laundry; and one should never have to look for the remote control or cordless phone.

The toilet lid should be down, the dirty clothes picked up, the paper brought in, and the dog taken out. I had a rule for everything!

I had my own little control business going, and I was the CEO.

"Why are you constantly looking for your keys? If you'd put them in one place, you wouldn't lose them."

"We can save so much money if we drive to Colorado instead of fly."

"Why would you want to see a movie? All you do is sit and stare at a screen. I don't want to go see a movie. I want to talk. *I want you to talk to me!*"

No wonder my poor husband wanted to go to the movies. He needed an escape from my controlling hand. It was a watershed moment for me when I realized how much of our communication revolved around my attempts to set him straight.

Your husband will be far more likely to talk to you if he doesn't feel manipulated or controlled. If he had a controlling mother, then this is especially distasteful to him, and you may have to be extra diligent in drawing him out and extra prayerful in asking God to show you when your controlling tendencies are on the verge of kicking in again.

All that is to say that loosening your grip on control may well be a factor in loosening your husband's lips. Learn to let go. Stop fighting for control. Stretch yourself. You'll be surprised at how good it feels.

Bottom Line: Wrestling matches aren't becoming for a woman.

chapter thirty-eight

STOP MOTHERING HIM

If you want to stifle a man's conversational interest, one of the quickest ways is to mother him. Men greatly dislike being mothered by their wives.

I (Connie) still remember asking my husband what he'd change about me if he could change only one thing. Without blinking he said, "I'd want you to stop mothering me." Ouch. Our husbands didn't marry us to be their mothers. They married us to be their wives, lovers, soul mates, and close friends.

Women tend to show love by mothering, but that's not how our husbands perceive it. What mothering says to them is that we doubt they can take care of themselves without our help. Mothering can turn into a control issue if left unchecked, and your husband may grow to resent you even more when this occurs.

Sarah is a friend of ours who struggled with this. She was a wonderful wife to her husband, and they shared a close relationship. And then they had children! As she mothered her three boys, she found that more often than not she simply extended her mothering skills to her husband as well. She directed the family activities: Each day she'd tell each of the "boys" what to do, what to wear, and when to be where.

As she trained her children, she threw her husband into the mix as well: Pick up your socks; take your dirty dishes to the dishwasher; and wipe the toothpaste out of the sink. She discovered that she became even more relentless toward her husband as time went by; surely if a six-year-old son could be trained in such matters, a forty-year-old man should be able to as well. Her expectations became higher and her frustration mounted, as did her husband's.

One evening her husband shared with her that he simply couldn't "work up" his love for her anymore. It was as if she had mothered the love right out of him.

Sarah began to stop mothering him and start loving him again—in the way she had when they were first married—when she thought he was the most wonderful man in the world. When she placed herself in this "demothering" mode, she ushered in a new era for the entire family. The boys love this new mother that doesn't nag their dad, and her marriage is warmer than it has ever been. Conversation is flourishing again, and her husband no longer has to worry about "working up" enough love for her. It is now there naturally.

Often women fall into the "mothering trap" and then later wonder what happened to the romance in their marriage. Seldom does a husband's "mother" notice that she has stopped being his sweetheart. A man will not feel particularly romantic toward a woman who acts like his mother. He doesn't need to be told what to wear, how to drive, what to eat, or when to go to bed—among other things. Try restricting your mothering to your children and their friends, and begin to see yourself as the captivating, intriguing woman your husband wants you to be.

Bottom Line: Men don't want their wives to act like their mothers.

chapter thirty-nine

GET YOUR PRIORITIES RIGHT

Who hasn't struggled with priorities in life? We certainly have.

If your husband feels he's a priority, he'll be much more likely to talk to you. What do you suppose would happen if you made him feel that he ranked right below God on your priority list? Undoubtedly he'd like it a lot—a whole lot.

It's so easy to get your priorities mixed up. Take a few minutes to see how you're doing in this area.

Rate each of these in the order of which they take priority in your life. (Note: Don't rate them according to what you *think* they should be, but what they honestly are.)

_____ Home
_____ Hobbies
_____ Social commitments
_____ Your spiritual life
_____ Husband
_____ Children
_____ Friends

_____ Church commitments
_____ Time for yourself
_____ Time with extended family
_____ Reading the newspaper and magazines

We don't know how you ranked each of these, but the one thing that stands out to us as we work with women is that their husbands are falling further and further down the list.

One of the areas that is most often the cause of a woman's priorities getting out of line is that of children. Oh, how we love our children! They are the feathers in our caps and the diamonds in our crowns. They put a sparkle in our eyes, a smile on our faces, and add freshness to our world.

Does *anything* compare to the high calling of being a godly mother? Yes! It's the high calling of being a godly wife! Yet so often our husbands are shunted aside as we make our children our number one priority. After a woman's relationship with God, her relationship with her husband should be her highest priority.

Let's take as an example a woman who bends over backward to assure that the quality of her children's lives is high. She's done this for them all of their lives. The children are now teenagers, and rather than teaching them how to do some of these things themselves (as should have been done years ago), she continues to do them all herself.

This is what a visiting friend might observe on a typical day:

The kids come home from school. Mom immediately begins scouring the refrigerator and pantry to see what she can come up with to feed them. One asks for a ham sandwich; another wants fresh veggies cut up and served with a special dip that she handmakes; and the third one decides he wants a mini-pizza. The friend says a mini-pizza is fine with her too.

Mother of the Year goes into overdrive. She dashes around the kitchen making all three dishes as her three children sit at the breakfast bar and ask her if she can go any faster. After all, they are hungry! No one makes any effort to help, nor does she ask. The friend sits quietly and observes everything. She is surprised to hear the kids continue to pressure their mother to go faster and to make their snack first. Even though it looks like it would be fun to live this way, something inside of her says otherwise. Her parents would never put up with her bossing them around like this.

Before long the mouthwatering snacks are put together, and each is placed in front of the appropriate child. They begin to munch their way through their food, and no one says thank you but the visiting child. Mom hovers about, asking if she can refill their glasses or make them anything else. About this time Dad arrives home from work early and asks what's going on.

"We're having a snack," says one of the teens.

"Wow, that looks awfully good," he says. "I believe I'll make me something."

"Why don't you ask your wife to make it for you?" the innocent friend suggests. "She fixed all this stuff for us. I bet she'd fix something for you, too." She couldn't imagine otherwise, for when her dad comes home from work her mother does this.

The man looks at the visitor in surprise. Obviously the child doesn't realize how this home operates. He smiles at her sweet suggestion and replies, "Oh, I'll make my own snack. My wife's specialty is taking care of the kids, not taking care of me."

His children continue eating as if nothing has been said. His wife, though, gives a derisive "harumph," frustrated that his comments reflected poorly on her in front of a visitor—even though they were the truth.

The man makes his own sandwich and then carries it into another room to eat as his wife sits at the kitchen counter, animatedly talking with the kids.

This scene is played out in hundreds of ways in the homes of families today. The tender part of a woman's heart that was once reserved for her husband is now given to her children. Certainly our children should have a tender part of our hearts, but it shouldn't come at our husband's expense, and it shouldn't replace the part that was meant to be his.

It might be helpful to pause and take a hard look at yourself. Have you unwittingly placed your children ahead of your husband? This can seem like such a sweet thing to do, but it violates your husband's rightful place in your life.

It is not the best thing for children either. So often women are determined to be their child's friend at all costs. If this is what you're doing, be aware that this "friendship" comes with a high price:

- a watered-down relationship with your husband,
- a child who will have very little, if any, respect for his father and, ultimately, you,
- a child that believes he can manipulate the system to get what he wants,
- a child with skewed priorities, often based on what he's seen modeled by you,
- a child who expects things to be handed to him on a silver platter,
- a child with a surly attitude and a poor work ethic,
- a self-centered child who will one day most likely be a self-centered mate.

When you raise a child like this, you are using what we call "short-term love."

This short-term love is often the cause of lifelong handicaps, which started out with the sweetest of intentions.

Here are some ways to begin realigning wayward priorities.

1. Begin calling your husband an endearing name. Many women do this with their children, but few do so with their husbands.
2. Make it a point to let your husband know you've thought about him throughout the day.
3. Several times a week, tell your children something you admire in their father.
4. Have a regular date night, and maintain it as a priority.

5. When you're tempted to think negatively about him, consciously choose to think about one of his strengths instead.
6. Avoid putting him down, especially in front of your children.
7. Begin to see yourself as his friend, wife, lover, and soul mate.
8. Seek your husband's advice and counsel. Invest in his stock.

Purpose to become a woman whose priorities are right. Dare to be countercultural in this regard—be a wife who puts her husband ahead of her children.

Bottom Line: God. Husband. Children. Family. Friends.

chapter forty

QUIT FEEDING THE MONKEYS

The last thing you want to do in your husband's life is create stress and conflict. He has enough of that to deal with without any additional contributions. You can be so rigid or set in your ways that you add havoc to your husband's life by being a martyr about doing everything.

What you want to do is feed your own monkey and let him feed his. What does this mean? If you begin feeding a monkey, he'll start looking to you as his food source. So if you don't want the responsibility of feeding him for the long haul, don't start feeding him in the first place.

For instance, perhaps your husband does the finances, but you think you could do a better job. He agrees to let you do them. Maybe he mows the lawn, but you don't like how he misses a few spots here and there, so you begin to mow it. He offers to help you grocery shop but picks up things that you don't really need, so you tell him that from now on you'll go by yourself. He tries to help by getting the kids dressed in the morning, but you don't like the outfits he picks out, so you relieve him of this opportunity as well. He's willing to clean the bathrooms on Saturday mornings, but he's not as thorough as you'd like him to be. So you start feeding the bathroom monkey again.

For some women this list is endless. They have more monkeys than they know what to do with, and they are all hungry. Ask yourself what's really important in life and what's not. Most things aren't. If your husband offers to help, accept it, and don't put your standards onto his way of doing things.

Bottom Line: Monkeys are cuter if you're not responsible for feeding them all.

chapter forty-one

INTRODUCE MYSTIQUE

Just saying the word leaves you with a sense of wonder, doesn't it? A woman of mystique is a rarity, and certainly a bit of mystery surrounds the few who possess this quality. Nothing will quite get your husband's attention or cause him to want to talk to you like this will.

A woman of mystique has an allure, an aura that's hard to define. She is open and warm and conducts herself with dignity and poise. She exudes a quiet confidence that isn't dependent on others' thoughts or opinions of her. She seems to know who she is and is comfortable in her own skin. She is positive and accepting of herself and others. Discipline, which often sounds boring and staid, is a cornerstone of her life. Yet she's not rigid or legalistic.

There is a fragrance about this woman that draws you to her. She seems to understand that people talk about what's important to them. Perhaps it is the way that she listens and responds. She has a way of making you feel singled out and special and responds in a manner that is uplifting and encouraging.

She has an unmistakable presence yet isn't brazen or provocative. Her beauty goes beyond the clothes she wears or the accessories that accompany them. A complete lady in every way, you sense by the way that she throws back her head and laughs that there is another side to her that is reserved for a select few.

She is a walking juxtaposition. She seems to be made of tenderness and steel at the same time. She exhibits graciousness at every turn yet is firm in her resolve and is uncompromising. She is not oblivious to problems, nor does she bury her head in the sand. She maintains a calm assurance that all will be well. She doesn't wring her hands in the face of adversity but has an abiding faith that comforts all around her.

Is she perfect? No. Is she fallible? Absolutely. Does she allow herself to be vulnerable? Of course. Does she err? No doubt. But at her core is a woman who wants to please God. This is what makes up the warp and woof of her life, and what sets her apart from those women who simply reflect worldly mystique.

While the daily rut of life can be the comfortable path to take, the magnetism and attraction that once was characteristic of your marriage can be slowly leached away. Allowing God into your life, and the process of growth that takes place in you as you walk with Him, will revitalize and renew you and refresh your marriage. This won't happen all at once, because it is a process that occurs over time as a woman allows God more and more control of her life.

When a woman reflects God in her life, her husband may be changed without her ever saying a word.[1] This is a work of God. And she will experience a brightened countenance and a richer walk as she journeys through life with the One who made her.

Begin today to become a woman of mystique. Pray, hope, have faith, love.[2] Place your hope and confidence in God, and become the woman He meant for you to become. This will undoubtedly pique your husband's interest, and he will wonder what's happening to you—and he will be thrilled to find out!

Bottom Line: Confidence in God is irresistible.

part four

About the Two of You

lighting the coals of communication

The greatest compliment that was ever paid me was when one asked me what I thought and then attended to my answer.

HENRY DAVID THOREAU

Are you ready to brush up on some long-neglected skills? In this section we will visit the world of interactive conversation between a man and his wife. These skills are easy to put into practice.

Perhaps you remember when you first got a computer. Wires were strewn here and there; instructions were nearby; the various components were before you; and finally it was connected. The first question on the mind of every neophyte computer person is, "How do I turn this thing on?" The next thing on the agenda is familiarizing oneself with the various programs, keys, and icons on the screen. You don't learn everything the first day, as you well know. It takes a while. But once you are up and running, you wonder how you ever got by without your computer.

The same is true when talking with a man. "How do I turn him on conversationally?" has got to be the question on the minds of the vast majority of married women. Learning how to listen well and how to approach various kinds of conversations are two of the basic skills that will help you as you interact with your husband.

The following chapters are about listening and about ways to say things that will create a climate that will encourage your husband to talk to you. If you put these ideas into practice, we don't think he will be able to resist the way that you are showing interest in him again—who he is, what he has to say, and what he thinks. He will undoubtedly notice that something is very different about you. You are looking at him when he is talking. You are responding to what he just said and not interjecting what you had on your mind. You no longer take offense at the way he says things. You now know how to get his attention and no longer expect him to read your mind.

What you will learn in this section is invaluable and will help you in all your other relationships as well. After all, who wouldn't want to talk to someone who is interested in what you have to say?

chapter forty-two

LEARN THE ABC'S OF LISTENING

Generally speaking, we believe there's a direct relationship between a woman's willingness to listen and a man's willingness to talk.

Men are task oriented. They don't speak just to speak. They will likely only speak if there's a reason to and if you are listening.

Honing your listening skills is an excellent way to encourage him to talk to you.

Here is an example. When your husband comes home at the end of the day, have you ever found yourself too engrossed in a dozen other things to know whether he said anything to you, let alone inquire about his day? Maybe you're exhausted, and listening to him is not how you want to spend your last thread of energy. You give just enough polite nods and comments to make him think you're listening. Ever done that? We have. Suffice it to say, this does nothing to encourage a husband to talk to his wife.

Here are seven helpful tips on listening:

1. Look at your husband when he speaks to you.
If your eyes are focused elsewhere, it will appear that your mind is elsewhere as well. Stop whatever it is you are doing, and look at your husband as he speaks.

2. Lean forward as you listen.
Being an "edge of your seat" listener shows him that you're being more than just kind, that you're very interested in what he's saying.

3. Give feedback.
Respond to his words by nodding and smiling. Ask questions. This lets him know that you were listening closely to what was said.

4. Don't interrupt or change the subject.
Wives are renowned for this! One of my (Connie) husband's friends once put his hand over my mouth because I was finishing too many of his sentences. Let your husband complete his own sentences, and allow him to finish talking about the subject he's discussing, even if it's not your favorite. Don't yawn, look at your watch, or glance around the room or out the door or window.

5. Repeat back to him some of the things he said.
This shows you were listening and is validating and confirming.

6. Compliment him on his insights and wisdom.
This will encourage him to continue sharing with you in the future.

7. Show your appreciation.
Thank him for sharing his thoughts with you. Men are wired differently and often don't realize how much it means to a woman for her husband to talk to her.

Rarely does someone listen with the intention of really hearing and thoughtfully evaluating what the speaker has just said. Instead it often seems as if people concentrate on what they are going to say next or how they want the conversation to go.

Could this be the reason your husband doesn't talk much? This was the case with Ann.

As we addressed this issue one night in our class, she wondered if it could be the situation in her marriage. Her husband had shut down almost entirely, and as she listened to us talk, she felt convinced that it was largely due to her poor listening skills. Between four kids, soccer schedules, aging parents, and working, it was a full-time job to keep all the balls in the air. Who had time for listening?

She weighed the situation and decided that she'd make time for it. In class we said that people invest themselves in pursuits they deem worthy, and she decided this was a worthy pursuit. She went home and without announcing to her husband what she was doing asked him a few simple questions and really listened to his answers.

She also remembered that much of their communication early on in their marriage used to take place when her husband came home from work. So the next evening when he walked through the door, she stopped stirring the spaghetti sauce and asked about his day. He was very brief in his report because he had been programmed to think that even though she asked, she really wasn't interested or listening. But now she was!

Feeling braver by the moment, she took his hand and led him to the kitchen table. "Let's sit for a minute because I want to hear all about it," she said. The next day she did the same thing. And the next. And the next. Two weeks later she came to class beaming. "You won't believe it!" she said. "My husband now walks through the door with a lilt in his step and a smile on his face. He loves to come home, and it seems he loves to talk to me, too."

We asked her why this was.

"I believe it's because I began listening to him again."

Listening means much more than you think. What you are really saying when you listen to your husband is:

- You are important to me.
- I value what you have to say.
- You are a priority to me.

- I care.
- Other things can wait, but this can't.
- I love you.

If you've not been blessed with the gift of listening, take heart! It can be learned by anyone who is willing to practice and make it a priority.

Bottom Line: Listening speaks volumes to your husband.

chapter forty-three

AVOID LISTENING PITFALLS

Do you see yourself in any of the following ways?

1. *The half-ear listener:* Just a small percentage of this woman's brain is really paying attention to what is being said. Most of her thoughts are elsewhere, especially if the conversation is about something in which she has no interest.
2. *The "even though I'm talking to the children, I'm still listening" listener:* This woman constantly talks to the kids while her husband is talking to her. This is frustrating and even mildly embarrassing to a man—or anyone.
3. *The "even though I'm on the phone, I'm still listening" listener:* Listening to a telephone conversation, even while you nod to your husband as he speaks does not score big points in the listening department.
4. *The "I can interpret two conversations at once" listener:* This is similar to the half-ear listener. Stop trying to listen to someone else's conversation, the radio, the TV, or whatever else while your husband is talking to you.

5. *The "don't let my reading the newspaper keep you from talking," listener:* If your eyes are focused somewhere besides his face, your mind probably is as well.
6. *The "walk in and out of the room while you're talking" listener:* "Wandering" indicates you aren't listening, even if you say, "I can still hear you." Don't expect him to keep talking if you're always walking in and out of the room. Doing this says, "What you're saying isn't really important to me."
7. *The "I'm going to just rest my eyes a bit" listener:* It is difficult to talk to someone with his or her eyes closed. If you are that tired, tell him, "Honey, I love it when you share your day with me, but I am so tired right now I can barely keep my eyes open, and I don't want to miss a single thing that you're saying. Would you tell me more about it in the morning?" Hold his hand or touch him as you drift off to sleep.
8. *The "I can do at least six other things while you're talking" listener:* Maybe you can, but you will be listening less attentively when you do. Your husband may or may not do this in return—most men listen differently and may putter as they listen. It shows honor and respect, however, to give others your complete attention when they speak, and you can choose to do this for your husband even if he doesn't listen in this way.
9. *The "interrupt constantly" listener:* Place your hand over your mouth if you have to, but let your husband have the luxury of finishing his sentences before saying anything yourself.
10. *The "I'll listen for thirty seconds" listener:* Don't dangle a carrot only to yank it away. If your husband is telling you something, listen! If for some reason you can't listen at that moment, tell him why and suggest a better time for you to talk with him.

Bottom Line: Don't allow not listening to become your pitfall.

chapter forty-four

DEVELOP GREAT RESPONSES

If your listening skills need shoring up, we suggest that you practice responding well. In order to respond, you have to listen to what is being said. As you begin to respond, your husband will begin to talk. Incidentally, you will not believe what a treasure learning to respond is until you see the reaction of not only your husband, but also everyone you know! Practice on your friends and children. They will love it.

Responding is an acquired skill. Here are some tips to help get you started:

- Tell him about something, and ask his opinion. Listen when he gives it, and make comments on what he just said.
- Ask questions the next time he talks to you, keying in on his answers.
- Interject praise and encouragement when you can. "Wow, honey! Way to go. I'm so proud of you for thinking on your feet like that."
- Initiate conversation about something that he's interested in. Has he just played a round of golf or helped develop a new approach to something at work? Is he serving on a committee

at church or coaching a Little League team? Discover what he's interested in, and then ask questions about it, giving back pertinent comments on what he has shared. Watch a good interviewer like Larry King. He says very little. His job is simply to draw his guest out.

- Don't demand that he talk. If he doesn't "take the bait," don't get mad or defensive. Don't accuse him of never talking to you or tell him you're tired of doing all the work.
- Interject a little playfulness from time to time. I (Nancy) once concocted my own version of *Who Wants to Be a Millionaire?* using topics I knew would interest Ray. He loved it! It started us talking that night as we lay in bed together, and we continue to laugh about it many months later.

We see listening as a low-cost stock that yields high dividends. It doesn't cost a thing to listen except for your time and a bit of practice. It often results in encouraging your husband to open up to you.

Open your ears and be focused! Soften your eyes and put on a smile. Stop what you're doing the next time your husband walks through the door, and ask him about his day. Begin drawing him out, and give him ample space to be himself without pressuring him to conform to your standards.

Bottom Line: Great responses stimulate conversation.

chapter forty-five

LISTEN TO HIS SILENCE

Silence may be golden, but it is often one of the most misunderstood issues in marriage. Most men don't mind silence, but wives frequently misunderstand this and think that something is wrong in the relationship when it occurs.

To a man, silence is okay and ordinarily indicates nothing beyond the silence itself.[1]

To a woman, silence indicates that something is lacking in the relationship. She frequently takes responsibility for his silence and assumes the role of "getting him out of it," when he actually may be enjoying the quiet moments that she is so concerned about. Until a woman begins to understand this, her attempts to get her husband to talk to her may be undermined.

Rita, an extroverted friend of ours who enjoys life to the hilt, found this occurring in her marriage. She said things would be going along just fine and then *boom!* her husband would grow quiet and pensive and seemed to withdraw from her. Rita couldn't figure this out. There never seemed to be a warning that preceded these stretches of silence—they came out of the blue. It was difficult for her not to take this personally. *Surely I've done something to irritate him, but what could it be?* she wondered.

Periodically she'd ask him, "Is everything okay, honey? You seem so quiet."

"Yes," he'd say. "Everything is just fine. I'm just being me."

"Have I made you mad or anything?" she'd push.

"No, I just need some peace and quiet."

This really bothered Rita. These silences made her uncomfortable, and she couldn't help but feel that she had done something to contribute to them.

Finally she talked to a good friend who had been married for many years. The woman smiled and put her arm around Rita. "Every man has a need for some silence in his life from time to time," she said. "Don't worry when this happens. Don't pester or nag or nitpick when it does. If he wants to talk to you about it later, he will. Give him his space and continue to be loving and warm. These times will pass."

This sage advice from an older woman helped Rita see things differently. She no longer felt threatened or intimidated. She no longer felt these periods of silence had anything to do with her. And indeed, once she left her husband alone with his thoughts, he usually shared them with her at a later time.

One of the best things you can do for your marriage is to learn to support and love your husband in his silences. This support is invaluable to a man—no expectations, no pressures, no hassles. He's free to be who he is.

Don't let this silence cause you to grow insecure in your relationship with him. Don't become fragile during these times or worry about what's going on. Worrying doesn't do any good![2] Also, don't ask him what's wrong over and over again. Take a step back and give him his space. Don't feel the need to take responsibility for his silence or think it's up to you to "get him out of it." He most likely just needs some time to himself.

We all need this from time to time, yet it can be difficult for a man to find. Most work all day and are the last ones home in the evenings.

If you sense this need in your husband's life, help carve out some space for him to be alone. Take the kids and go to the park. Call a friend and go on a walk. Don't begrudge his need for silence. Respect it, and don't put your life on hold when he's in a quiet mode.

A man especially appreciates a wife who remains warm and gracious through his quiet moments.

Bottom Line: Silence can be golden if you don't insist it be otherwise.

chapter forty-six

LIGHTEN HIS LOAD

Another great thing you can do when you're wondering if everything is okay with your husband is to ask him if there's anything you can do to lighten his load. Maybe you've never asked him this in your life. Maybe it will shock the socks right off of him. But he'll enjoy being barefoot for a change.

Here's how you do it:

- look him in the eyes,
- take his hand,
- open your mouth,
- and say these words: "Is there anything I can do to lighten your load?"

This is a big deal to a man. He is besieged with all sorts of pressures, many of which you can't begin to imagine. Pressures are different for a man than they are for a woman, and men have a tendency to internalize them rather than to talk about them. When you offer to lighten your husband's load, you're offering to depressurize his life a bit. You're saying to him that you care about him without saying a word directly about it; you're letting him know that you've noticed he seems to be on overload and you want to help.

What this does is invite your husband to talk about what's going on in his life. You don't have to go a single step down the road of, "What is wrong with you? Why can't you learn to handle stress better? It's a part of life so just get used to it. I am stressed myself, and you are making me crazy. I wish you would straighten up and fly right. Would you like me to give you some flying lessons on coping right now?"

If you want to take things a step further, frequently ask him in the mornings before he heads out if there's anything you can do for him that day to lighten his load. This is a demonstration of commitment to your man, an offer to interrupt your schedule for his needs. What you're saying is simple, but what your husband is hearing is *love* with a capital *L*. Men who hear love with capital letters are far more apt to talk to their wives than those who don't.

Bottom Line: Use capital letters when you spell.

chapter forty-seven

USE MARS PROTOCOL

Not long ago my (Connie) youngest daughter, along with a dozen or so other sixth graders, was doing a four-week study about Mars. It culminated in a trip to Des Moines, Iowa, where they visited a simulated space station. After the study was finished they put on a program demonstrating what they had learned.

Did you know that whenever you're in a spaceship and have something to say to the people on the ground (or vice versa), there is a certain protocol you go through to insure that they're receiving the information? It goes something like this:

"Mars, we have information for you. Are you ready to receive? Please acknowledge."

No further information is given until the astronauts acknowledge the sender's message and indicate that they are ready to receive. Once this occurs, additional information is exchanged.

The sixth graders showed us how to do this.

"Mars," the girls would say, "we have information for you. Are you ready to receive? Please acknowledge."

No response.

"Mars, we have information for you. Are you ready to receive? Please acknowledge."

No response but a little static, as if Mars was beginning to wake up from a nap.

"HELLO, MARS! ARE YOU THERE? WE HAVE INFORMATION FOR YOU. ARE YOU READY TO RECEIVE? PLEASE ACKNOWLEDGE."

"Oh, hi, space station. Yes, we are ready to receive. Go ahead."

When the boys sent information to the girls, the girls responded the first time. But when the girls had information to send to the boys, it took a few attempts to get the boys' attention and then to get them to respond. We had to chuckle because it seems this is the way communication occurs in life in general.

Let's take a look at how Mars protocol operates in a marriage. So often a woman jumps off into a conversation and thinks her husband is tracking, because if he jumped off into a conversation she'd be tracking.

Not only is her husband not tracking; he's not even aware that he's not tracking. "You never listen to me," she then accuses.

"Yes, I do," he defends himself.

"No, you don't, and here's a perfect example of it," she shouts back.

"I didn't even know you were talking to me," he says, even though he may have been the only person in the room.

"Who did you think I was talking to—the wall?" she asks indignantly.

"No, I just didn't realize you were talking to me," he replies honestly.

Some people spend their lives this way. The wife is constantly frustrated that her husband doesn't listen to her, and all the husband can figure out is that her frustration has something to do with him, but just what he's not sure.

One of the keys to good communication is to make sure Mars is ready to receive when you're ready to talk. Don't assume he is—ask him to acknowledge that he is. If he's not and you continue talking, you're wasting your breath and your nerves.

With this in mind, there are ways you can help your husband hear you—ways to help Mars acknowledge and receive. We've listed a few below:

1. Use *would,* not *could,* when asking a man to do something. Women use *could* because it seems more polite. It's as if you're asking them to do something instead of telling them to. But men prefer the direct approach. This was next to impossible for me (Connie) to do, because *would* seemed so bossy.

Whenever I asked my husband if he "could" do such and so, it drove him wild. "Of course I CAN do it," he'd say. "What you really want to know is if I WOULD do it. Say what you mean. Don't hint about it and expect me to take the bait."

His answer seemed rather harsh to me. Rather harsh? Actually, it seemed brutal. But this is how he felt about it. So I began retraining myself to ask in that way, and found it amazingly easy to do. It worked so well that I playfully suggested I leave out the word *would,* and simply issue a direct order: "Go to the store and buy a loaf of bread." Talk about saying what you mean! Even he agreed that this was cutting it a bit too close for him. Interject fun as you work out the differences between you.

2. Say what you think. Don't give clues—even big ones—and expect him to grab onto them and read your mind. Women are often able to do this, but men aren't. Tell him plainly and simply what you think.

3. Be concise and to the point. Men don't care if the drapes are pink or purple or neon orange, or that the sweater Betsy was wearing was hand-knit by a woman for whom his mother once baby-sat. In Italy. In 1950. Spare him the details unless he's a detail-loving man, which would be quite rare.

4. When asking for his input, make certain you understand what he means, and if you don't, ask until you do.

My (Nancy) husband once said, "Get any color carpet you want, I just don't care. I'll like what you like!" So I bought olive green carpet, which looked beautiful with gold and orange (it was the '70s). Ray came home after it was installed and said, "What's this? It looks like an oil slick from a capsized cargo ship!" This was not good news.

Thankfully he was promoted shortly after that and we moved to another city. We left the olive green carpeting and hoped the Joneses enjoyed it more than Ray had. In this case I had asked Ray and he gave his input. But now I would probably bring a piece of the carpeting home for him to see just to be sure—even though he said he didn't care.

5. Don't accuse him of not listening to you. This makes him feel demeaned and childish. And it makes you look like a controller. Keep your story short, and assume that he's listening.

6. Realize that women place a higher value on listening than most men do. To a woman, it's another way of expressing love and is reflective of the relationship. To a man it's more something you do, more a task.

7. Thank him when he has listened to you. Men need this kind of validation, especially in the area of communication. They often feel they're on a slippery slope and can't quite figure out what it is their wives want and need. Help your husband feel more confident by noticing and praising his efforts. This will make him more willing to take risks the next time.

8. Share with your friends or family (when he can hear you) what a great listener he is. He'll feel fabulous, and before long he'll begin to think of himself as a good listener as well.

Bottom Line: Speak astronaut.

chapter forty-eight

DON'T EXPECT HIM TO READ YOUR MIND

The mind is a complex wonder of nature. It enables an individual to feel, perceive, will, and reason. It enables a person to store infinite bits of important information, as well as enough trivia to solve crossword puzzles. It is the storehouse of the memory, and because it keeps things you have learned tucked away, you can still remember how to do things that you haven't done for years—like ride a bike and not fall off. It can hold more than one language, remember countless voices, detect various dialects, and enable you to respond to a baby's cry in the middle of a sound sleep.

How in the world can we expect our husbands to read it?

Not long ago I (Connie) was feeling blue about something and was moping around the house. After a while my husband said, "Honey, is there anything wrong?"

As is often the case for women, I didn't come right out and say, "Yes, something is wrong, and I'm feeling totally overwhelmed by it." Instead I sighed deeply and said in a quiet sort of tone, "Oh, I don't know."

My husband looked at me to see if I was finished or not. Since I didn't say anything else, he assumed that either nothing was wrong or that I didn't want to talk about it. If I didn't know what was wrong, he surely wasn't going to be able to figure it out either. So he went back to what he was doing.

I watched him walk out of the room and was shocked. Wasn't he going to pursue my deep sighing and heavily intoned "Oh, I don't know"? Apparently not! This made me even bluer. Didn't he care that I was discouraged? Now not only was I discouraged over the original issue; I was hurt that he hadn't made more of an effort to draw me out. And it didn't help that he was now out in the garage happily blowing the leaves out of the corners.

Women have a tendency of not saying what we really mean. Instead we dance around the issues—sending out subtle signals that we think are clearly telling our husbands what to do next. Men don't understand these vague signals—they understand signals that are direct and to the point. While a woman can read another woman's signals, men can't. They aren't even aware signals are being sent. They're not women.

Had I said this same thing ("Oh, I don't know") to a female friend, she would have said to me, "Oh, Connie, I can tell you are really upset about something. Why don't I fix you a hot cup of tea while you tell me what's going on?" Her gentle prompting would have made me feel loved and nurtured and would have told me that she was truly interested in what was going on in my life. At that point, I would have begun to share with her what was making me blue.

Men don't work that way. Most don't understand that a woman tends to "test the waters" to see if he's going to be receptive and involved in what she's about to say. If she determines that he is, she'll continue to share her feelings. Most of the time, though, she'll discover that he's not taking the bait. This isn't because he doesn't want to; it's because he doesn't know to.

The secret, then, is to stop testing the waters with your husband. Get in the habit of saying what you mean and meaning what you say. This is what men do and what they assume you'll do in return.

In the past both of us have sulked around our houses for days, waiting for our husbands to "discover" we're upset and then "persuade" (i.e., encourage, urge, beg) us to talk about what's going on. When they asked us if anything was wrong, of course our answer was no, but we spoke in a hurt voice that we thought said everything to the contrary.

The hurt voices usually went over their heads. What they heard was no, and that's what they acted on—which only made us more frustrated.

"Do we have to spell it out for them?" we'd wonder to ourselves. Well, in a word, yes, we did. It was years before we learned that what they needed to hear from us was the truth! "Yes, I am upset. (Wow, that was so easy to say!) Can we talk about it?" This is music to a man's ears—not the fact that his wife is upset, but the fact that she'll say what she's thinking and not expect him to read her mind.

One of the best ways to remove the walls in your marriage is to stop expecting him to read your mind. Men aren't mind readers! This fact will not surprise any woman reading this book. But you can help him read your mind, in a sense, by saying what you mean up front.

Bottom Line: Words are the window to your soul, and without them the shades are drawn.

chapter forty-nine

HOW TO ASK FOR HELP

Men and women ask for help in completely different ways. If you want your husband's help, learn to speak his language. This will save you a lot of time, frustration, and energy—not to mention aspirin and antacid, too!

Approach your husband without pointing your finger or assigning blame.

Don't overwhelm him with an emotional onslaught of how he's not doing his part. Men don't like sudden onslaughts of conversation anyway, especially if they are negative and directed toward themselves.

Be low-key, nonthreatening, and nonaccusatory. Begin by telling him how *you* feel. Keep the focus on you and how you're feeling. Don't intimate that it's his fault. How can it be his fault if he has no idea how you're feeling (and truly, he probably doesn't)?

Don't begin your sentences with "You don't," "You always," or "You never."

Tell him—without blaming—how overwhelmed and discouraged you feel, and then ask if he'd be willing to help you.

Let him see your genuine concern for the relationship. If you do this, most likely he will rally around. Believe it or not, most husbands see themselves as noble men who like rescuing their princesses from fire-breathing dragons (in this case, the jaws of mental and emotional overload and drain).

Make certain you've examined your own heart before doing this, though, for if he senses any self-serving purposes or manipulation in your request, he won't be open.

Have a back-and-forth conversation. Resist the urge to do all the talking. Lay out the problem, as you see it, and ask his help in solving it. Again, and we can't say this enough, if he thinks that what you're doing is pointing your finger at him, he'll become defensive and won't cooperate. The key is to keep the focus on the issue at hand.

Imagine going to your banker and saying to him, "My checking account is running on empty! No matter how many deposits I make it seems the demand for money exceeds the amount that is put into it. Can you help me solve the problem?"

Of course the banker would tell you to either decrease your spending or increase your deposits. This is basically what you're asking your husband to do. Suggest ways he can deposit a little more into your account (i.e., take the kids to school, pick up his cleaning on the way home, take his parents out for time alone when they visit, etc.), as well as decrease the spending (i.e., offer to pick up pizza for dinner one night a week, take the kids to the park so you can get the house organized, help you write checks for the bills, etc.).

It helps many couples to write down a plan of attack. Then it is not as likely to get pushed to the back burner, and things won't fall into the old pattern quite so soon. Some have even posted the plan on the inside of their closets or placed it alongside their alarm clocks. This way it's fresh on their minds, and they can refer to it often.

Remember to be specific. In fact, it is almost impossible to be too specific in this area. Even the simplest plan stands a better chance of succeeding if it is in written form. Don't criticize him the second he forgets to do something. Give each other time, and help each other out as you do. Adjust the plan as needed.

Ask him if there are things he feels overloaded or worried about.

You may be surprised at his answer. Often we become so focused on our own sense of feeling overwhelmed that we don't realize our husbands may be feeling the same way with different issues. They aren't as apt to bring these up unless you ask specifically. Asking about this is a super way to show your husband your love and support.

If your husband is open to it, pray together about the situation. There is something that brings a couple closer when they bring their requests before God to ask for His insight and wisdom as they deal with the situation.

Change takes time! Don't become discouraged or frustrated if you fall back into your old patterns from time to time. When you find yourself doing this, begin back at square one.

Bottom Line: If you need help, ask for it.

chapter fifty

"IF I HAVE TO ASK, IT DOESN'T COUNT"

A practical way to build communication in your marriage is to do away with the phrase, "If I have to ask, it doesn't count."

Here's the deal. If a man thought like you did, then you wouldn't have to ask him to do things. Men don't plot to drive their wives crazy by deciding to wait until they're asked to do something before they do it. They simply aren't thinking about it at all until they've been asked.

Stop for a moment and think about this. It will revolutionize the way you see your husband. Women tend to think that men cop out in this regard. A woman cannot understand why she should have to ask her husband to do something that so obviously needs doing. The crux of the matter is that it's only obvious to her, as hard as that is to believe. It's not obvious to him.

A few years ago, I (Connie) remember rushing around the kitchen trying to get the girls off to school and myself out the door as well. One of the girls needed a lunch; one needed a form filled out and signed; and the third wanted me to braid her hair. I was frazzled, and the day was still young. About this time my husband walked into the kitchen in his robe—he had worked late the night before—sat down on the couch, and began glancing at the headlines in the morning's paper.

Surely he'll see me running around like a chicken with my head cut off and offer to help, I thought. He didn't. As I continued my headless chicken impersonation—was that sweat pouring from my brow?—I noticed that my husband seemed more engrossed than ever in the paper.

My blood pressure tripled in about two seconds, and I said (rather coolly I'm afraid), "Do you think you could help me in here?"

"Help you do what?" he asked innocently, looking up from the paper.

"Sign papers, make lunches, braid hair, carry projects, and find my sanity," I responded in a clipped tone.

He raised his eyebrows. Certainly he knew the chill in the air couldn't be attributed to the summertime weather outside.

"Sure," he said. "All you have to do is ask."

I looked at him in disbelief. I thought I could see the vein in my neck pulsating out past my chin. Now not only did I have to sign papers, make lunches, braid hair, carry projects, and find my sanity, I also had to ask him to help me out. I could tell he was completely serious.

Well, so was I! "If I have to ask, it doesn't count," I said. "How can you sit and read the paper and not notice that things are rather hectic in here?"

"Connie," he said calmly (which did nothing for my blood pressure), "if you have to ask, ask. Stop waiting for me to read your mind, because it's not going to happen." (And I can assure you that it hasn't happened yet!)

For the umpteenth time—and as much for our benefit as for yours—we repeat: Men aren't wired like women. In the above scenario, a woman would walk into the kitchen, see the chaos going on and immediately pick up a knife and begin spreading peanut butter and jelly. Men, however, walk into the same room, see the morning paper, and wonder who won the football game last night. They don't realize there is a domestic crisis brewing right under their noses.

It's not that your husband doesn't want to help; it's that he doesn't realize you need it.

Men like it when you not only ask them to help, but tell them what to do. You might say, "Oh, the cavalry has arrived, and you're it! Would you finish putting these notes in Jodi's folder while I make the lunches?" Now you've let him know you're stressed, and you've done it in an upbeat way. Plus you've told him how he can help.

A friend who is associated with the military said recently, "We men don't aim to drive our wives nuts by being clueless; it's simply that we depend on them to provide us with the clues. The more specific they are, the clearer our mission becomes. We like missions, especially well-defined ones. But if the mission is poorly defined or not defined at all, we'll miss the fact that one even exists."

Five reminders:

1. If you have to ask, ask!
2. If you have to ask, it still counts!
3. Don't berate him for "making" you have to ask.
4. Define the mission.
5. Show your appreciation for what he's done, even if you had to ask him to do it. Men like appreciation—remember that it's what motivates them. Your genuine thankfulness will often spur him to want to help you again in the future—even though you may have to ask first!

Bottom Line: Expect to ask for your husband's help. That's usually the only way he knows it's needed.

chapter fifty-one

IF AT FIRST YOU DON'T SUCCEED

What do you do if you ask your husband to do something and he continues to forget? Most women make the mistake of asking again and again, becoming louder and more hostile each time. This quickly elevates itself to all-out nagging, making your husband feel demeaned, defensive, and mothered.

The better approach is to continue asking your husband to do whatever it is you're wanting, but in the same kind, gentle tone you used the first time. When you do this, you take yourself out of the position of full-time nag and mother, and you remain his loving, helpful wife. Sound impossible? It's not! In fact, you'll be surprised at how this approach will motivate him to want to do the chore.

One of the first times I (Connie) tried this was by asking my husband to look at what appeared to be a leak under the kitchen sink. He said he would.

A few days later the cabinet was still moist, and I was sure he'd forgotten to take a look at it.

"Honey, when you get a minute, would you take a peek under the sink?" I asked him, as though I hadn't mentioned it before.

"I am so sorry," he said. "I totally forgot about it."

A few days later the leak still hadn't been looked at.

"I know you're so busy," I said with complete sincerity (and no sighing or eye-rolling), "but when you get a minute, would you take a look under the sink?"

That did it. He stopped what he was doing and looked at the sink—partly, I believe, because I hadn't upped the ante to a full-scale war by shaming him into doing what I wanted him to do, when I wanted him to do it.

Too often women use this patient approach with their children instead of their husbands. Their children get multiple opportunities to do what's asked with little or no consequence. How often have you heard a mother say to her child, "Don't interrupt me when I'm talking," only to have the child continue to interrupt at an unprecedented rate? The mother continues to gently remind her child not to interrupt until she can finally give him her full attention, never getting mad or upset once and often even giving into the child.

When she asks her husband to do something, though, and he doesn't follow through, often there are immediate consequences. Remember, your job is to train your children, not your husband.

Give your husband the benefit of your patience, and simply ask again.

Bottom Line: Patience is a virtue—especially when you're asking your husband to do something!

chapter fifty-two

FRAME YOUR WORDS

Breathes there a man with a soul so dead that never to himself has he said, "I think there was a better way of saying that"?

There is, of course, a better way. It's presenting your thoughts in such a way that it blesses the listener and encourages dialogue. It's called "framing," and it can change your marriage.

There is more than one way to state the truth.

My (Nancy) husband often leaves his old tennis shoes in our sunroom. These are the ones he mows the lawn in, as well as washes the car in. Sometimes I toss these shoes behind a chair that sits in the corner. When he asks me where they are, I could state it two different ways:

- "Those shoes are sweaty and dirty. I hate them sitting at the entryway so I put them behind the chair."
- "Darling, the spiders behind the little chair in the sunporch were bored. Your shoes provided a tiny jungle gym for them to play in!"

You may be thinking, *That is ridiculous!* But didn't the frame on the second example make you smile, and didn't it get the point across in a slightly amusing way?

Another day I was having company from out of town and was feeling rushed. I said to Ray, "Would you consider doing me a huge favor? I cannot begin to tell you how helpful it would be to me. I would be so thankful if you would consider it."

Ray began to look nervous and surely wondered what could mean so much to me. I asked him if he would go to the neighborhood grocery store, which is about six blocks away, to pick up a few things for lunch. He gladly agreed, probably relieved that such a huge buildup was over something so small. But it wasn't small to me. I was simply framing my request in such a way that he would know what it meant to me.

Ray might ask, "How do I look in light gray?" Instead of saying that it makes his face take on an ashen tone that looks anemic, I would probably say, "You look so much better in brown. It goes with your eyes and makes them stand out." These statements are both true, but the truth can be framed so that feelings are left intact.

A husband who had been unemployed for quite some time was about to be hired. He said to his wife, "Do you think I will be able to function in the business world?"

Without hesitating she replied, "Of course! Your talents and skills have never been greater. You couldn't lose what you have learned over the years any more than you could forget how to ride a bicycle. You've also gained wisdom and perspective that can only grow through testing! I have never been more proud of you."

He was rallied by her words, which were beautifully framed in truth and love.

She who loves a pure heart and whose speech is gracious will have the king for her friend.[1] What an amazing statement this is! We are not looking to have kings for friends, but surely we all want to have our husbands as our friends.

Even your responses can be framed in a certain way to bless the listener. I (Connie) still remember an incident that took place many years ago at a bagel shop. My family and I were there for breakfast, and Wes told a joke. Either it was too early in the morning or he didn't tell the joke correctly, because it fell flat as a pancake. I saw our three daughters look at each other in amusement, as if to say, "Dad and his jokes." I had a choice to make: I could either side with them or bless my husband.

Unfortunately I sided with the girls and made a comment about how corny the joke was. What little air was left in his balloon suddenly escaped. What a terrible choice! Not because it impacted national policy or world peace, but because I held the power to either bless my husband's efforts or pour cold water on his spirit. And I chose the latter.

My response could have been framed so much better. I could have just as easily said, "Sweetheart, I just love it when you tell a joke"—because I do. "You are so funny and you make me laugh"—because he is and he does. Even if his joke fell flat that morning, I could have blessed him by my response and also modeled for my daughters what loyalty to one's mate looks like. And I would have been blessed myself as well.[2]

Words can heal and can also give hope and strength to the listener. Words must be chosen with great care. The tongue has been compared to a fire.[3] When fire is under control, it warms us. It is a source of cooking our food. It generates power to turn the wheels of industry.

When the tongue is out of control, however, the results can be devastating. They can burn through a home, and even though there may be survivors, they often walk wounded.

Ask the Lord to guard your words. Think twice before you speak, and consider how you might frame what you have to say in a way that blesses. You can't take words back.

Bottom Line: Framing your "painting" with grace and love causes its value to increase.

chapter fifty-three

PAINT YOUR WORDS

We mentioned word pictures earlier in the book and wanted to revisit them briefly because they can be such a powerful way to communicate with a man.

Word pictures are simply words you use to paint a picture. This helps your husband to better understand what you are trying to say. What you do is use words, phrases, and ideas that he can understand.

For instance, let's say you and your husband are invited to the home of an aunt whom you love deeply. Your husband, though, doesn't know her well and rarely sees her. He doesn't want to go and suggests you go alone. You know this would hurt your aunt because you know how much your aunt loves you and desires to get to know your husband.

You might paint a word picture like the following: "Honey, imagine if the CEO of your company invited us out to dinner. Of course you would go and want me to come along. But since I don't know him very well and hardly ever see him, I tell you to go alone. How would that make you feel?"

This made your husband see things completely differently.

Not long ago, as we were finishing this book, my (Connie) husband decided he wanted me to learn some of the intricacies of a computer. I had been up since two in the morning, as the deadline was bearing down. It was now about eight at night, and I was exhausted.

"Wes," I said to him, "imagine breaking a couple of eggs into a skillet. Then imagine frying them for three hours. Now think about turning them over and frying them for three more hours on the other side. Can you imagine what those poor eggs would look like? That's how my brain feels right now. Could you teach this to me tomorrow, when I'm fresh?"

"Of course," he said. "I'd be glad to. I had no idea you were that tired."

Dee Brestin, a fellow author and friend, tells of flying to Thailand with her husband to adopt their daughter.

In addition to being a wife and mother, Dee was a speaker, author, friend, mentor, and about three dozen other things. This was their fifth child—they already had a family back in Nebraska that this young girl would be joining.

On the way home her husband said to her, "Dee, did you see all the boys in that orphanage that needed a home?"

She asked her husband to look out the window at the plane's wing. He did. Then she asked him to imagine her hanging on to it for dear life. That, she told him, was how she felt right then. Her husband suddenly understood.

Try using word pictures to let your husband know how you're feeling and encourage him to use them with you as well. They can be an effective means of communication.

Bottom Line: Word pictures often say what regular words can't.

chapter fifty-four

"AM I STILL YOUR DARLING?"

Don't constantly ask your husband if everything is okay or if anything is wrong. In general, men take it to mean that *you* think things aren't okay.

This is a difficult concept for a woman to understand, because it's the caring side of her that motivates her to ask the question. She likes to be asked if she's okay—it shows care and concern to her. But to a man doing this shows nagging, mothering, and doubt—none of which a man is fond of. I (Connie) used to ask my husband this question all the time because he seemed so quiet (he's a doer, not a talker).

"Are you okay?" I'd ask.

"Well, I *was*," he'd reply, accenting the last word. I didn't know then how much men in general dislike this; certainly he did.

Instead, try developing a code word or phrase that asks him if everything is okay without irritating him. For instance, after several years of marriage, my (Connie) husband began calling me "darling." I was startled at first; I looked around to see if there was someone else in the room. He had never used endearing names before. I warmed up to this pet name very quickly and even began signing my e-mail to him with the letter *d* for darling, instead of my standard *c*.

A few days later, he was irritated about something. Instead of asking, "Are you okay?" as I had been doing, I said, "Am I still your darling?" He had to laugh, even though he was miffed about something I'd forgotten to do.

"Am I still your darling?" has become a code phrase between us. He knows I'm asking if everything is all right, but somehow it doesn't irritate him like the old way used to. And even if something's bothering him, everything seems better when he reassures me that I'm still his darling.

Another friend of ours says to her husband: "Would you like to go fishing?" This means, "Do you need to get away?" or "Do you need time alone?" Sometimes she says this in the dead of winter. Of course he's not going to go fishing in subzero weather, but this adds a touch of humor and lets him know that she's really asking if all is well.

Couples who cultivate their own private language (even if one is doing most of the cultivating) seem to connect more intimately than those who simply use normal English.

Bottom Line: Develop a private language with your husband.

chapter fifty-five

ANNOUNCEMENTS DON'T WORK

If there were a book entitled *The Ten Best Ways to Kill an Evening,* announcements would be right at the top. Ways *not* to start a conversation include:

- "We have to talk."
- "There are a few things you need to know."
- "There is something I've wanted to tell you for a long time."
- "There are a few issues that I need to get settled."
- "We need to schedule some time to discuss some problems."
- "I have something I need to discuss with you. Now."

Announcements are for airports, impending tornadoes, and national disasters. They shut men down. Flags go up and men become defensive. They go into "battle mode." Even the most sensitive man in the world becomes territorial and instead of listening becomes a lawyer—his client is himself. So often we wives become prosecutor, judge, and jury. We often have prolific evidence to present, especially if we are scorekeepers. Why do we think that our husbands are open to such an encounter?

Events like these have a driving force behind them. It is the failure to deal with problems simply and sweetly on the spot.

I (Nancy) had one such experience recently. Ray had taken the day off, and I left for work. He mowed the lawn, washed his car, vacuumed, and tidied our home. When I came home I put my things down on our dining-room table, much to his dismay, and he told me not to clutter the table. I picked them up and moved them, still cheerful and appreciative of all he had done. He then asked me where my tote bag was because he wanted to take it on a trip the next day. He went to the car to retrieve it, only to find it filled with my things. As he began to empty it, he was a bit irritated with me that I had several throwaway items in the bag. He let me know that he thought I should be a bit neater.

I didn't say anything, but I began to take into account wrongs suffered.[1] He then asked me a question about work; I began to respond in depth. By now, wearied by a long day of taking care of our home, he said that he could no longer listen to me and went to watch a show that was on TV, cutting me off mid-sentence.

With that last bit of news, instead of lovingly discussing the three things on my list, I announced, "*We have to talk.*" Ray was not the least bit interested in setting things right, and told me so. He has never responded well to such a statement from me.

And as I mulled this over, I realized I am the same way. I don't like it when someone calls me and says, "Can we get together? I have to talk to you." Immediately my guard goes up, and I am thinking of endless possibilities. Have I been offensive? Did I say something that she took the wrong way?

Now when someone makes an announcement like that to me, I ask him or her to tell me the reason. There is something about not knowing the direction that the conversation will take that is unsettling, to say the least.

Knowing that no one cares for announcements like that, I should have handled it differently. Four alternatives immediately come to mind. I could have:

- Ignored his edginess, realizing that he had done a monumental amount of work and that he was simply worn out.
- Apologized for messing up our clean house.
- Remembered that Ray has never/will never like long accounts of any story.
- If I felt that strongly about it, I could have talked this over with him when I wasn't annoyed and he wasn't tired.

Ray and I never did talk about it. He forgot, and it was no longer important to me.

If you want conversation to flourish, don't make announcements. They cause even the warmest man to freeze up.

Bottom Line: If you want your husband to look forward to your announcements, make sure that what you're announcing is good news.

chapter fifty-six

DON'T GO ON AND ON

Don't go on and on to a man about something that he can neither change nor do anything about. This is one of the quickest ways to shut your husband down. Remember, most men love figuring things out, and if there's no solution to what you're talking about, he'll become increasingly frustrated and upset.

For example, he can't change the fact that two of your best friends don't enjoy each other's company. He can't cure health problems. He can't magically make more money appear for new carpet. The more you continue to talk about these things, though, the more he feels he "should" be able to do something about them. Even though you are talking simply to be heard, he feels like he should "fix" whatever it is you're talking about. Not being able to fix your problem makes him feel bad, especially if it's something that's wearing on you emotionally.

On those occasions when you feel the need to talk about something he can't fix, gently say to him, "Honey, what I'm about to say has nothing at all to do with you, and I don't expect you to fix anything. You're the best fixer in the world, but all I want you to do right now is just let me talk about it. If I get sad or teary-eyed, don't feel bad. It's not about you. It's about me. There's nothing you need to do to make me feel better except let me talk."

When you do this, you let your husband off the hook right from the start. He can now listen to you without shifting into his Mr. Fix-It mentality. He can listen in a relaxed manner knowing he's not expected to come up with a solution. Once you've talked about it, try not to bring it up over and over again, or he'll step back into the "I should be able to fix this for her" mode.

Conversely, when your husband talks to you about something, he would like it very much if you could "fix" whatever he's complaining about. He wants you to do something regarding his complaint. He doesn't want you to simply be a listener. Men are doers; when they air a problem, they hope to benefit from your doing, not your being.

Say for instance that your husband is complaining that he ordered a pair of shoes from a catalog and they're too small. "Why don't they make their shoes in standard sizes?" he grumbles. He is not hinting at anything, merely talking about his problem. What he'd love to hear from you is, "Hey, baby, this is not a problem. Why don't I tape this box back up for you, fill out the return form, swing by the post office tomorrow, and get it returned?"

Talk about instant makeovers! Your husband will go from being Mr. Barracuda to Mr. Isn't Life Great and Aren't You Wonderful! You've just solved his problem, and he is now a happy camper.

Perhaps you're thinking, *Why do I have to take care of his error? I've got a busy life myself. I don't have time to box up his shoes and take them back. He ordered the wrong size; he can return the wrong size. He doesn't offer to return my stuff, so I'm not going to return his.*

Why concern yourself with who has done what for whom? Why not commit to being there for him and helping him out when you can? There is something about a helpful spirit that causes your husband to soften toward you and want to talk to you.

Not long ago, I (Connie) returned a humidifier to the store. My husband had bought it hoping it would be really loud and drown out the noise when he slept. The humidifier turned out to be quiet as a mouse, so he didn't want it.

One day as I approached our room, I could hear him letting out a long sigh. "What's up?" I asked. I rounded the corner and saw that he was boxing up the humidifier.

"I've never heard such a quiet humidifier in my life. Now I've got the hassle of taking it back," he grumbled. He carried it to the kitchen and set it by the back door.

I had not wanted him to get it in the first place. I didn't think it would do what he thought it would, plus it was large and took up valuable space in our small bedroom. The last thing I wanted was to take it back because I had tried to tell him these things in the first place.

I could either declare victory, breaking my arm patting myself on the back, or I could help my husband.

So the following day I put the box into my van and took it back. I didn't say a word about it to him. That night as I was drifting off to sleep, he leaned over and took my hand and thanked me—not just for taking back the humidifier, but for other things, too.

Taking the humidifier back took about twenty minutes, but I promise you that I'm still reaping the rewards of doing it even as I sit here and type, weeks later.

We hear so much about "enabling" these days. No one wants to enable another lest she lose a part of herself in the process. It seems to us that often this is an excuse women use to do only what they want and to refuse to do what they don't want to do. Consider what God would have you do in your role of wife, and then do it. Forget the media, TV shows, magazine articles, and everything else. Forget this book, for that matter. Ask God to show you how to be the kind of wife He wants you to be. Then be that kind of woman and wife.

Bottom Line: When your husband complains and grumbles, consider it a royal invitation. Small acts of service frequently soften even the stoniest of hearts.

chapter fifty-seven

DEVELOP THICKER SKIN

We did a survey of three hundred men to determine why men don't talk more readily to their wives. The number one answer given by these men was that their wives overreact when they speak.

Here's a simple test to determine your level of touchiness:

- Do your feelings get hurt more than once a day?
- Do you want to "get even" with people who hurt your feelings?
- Do you hold onto grudges longer than a day?
- Do you readily accept the apologies of those who offend you?
- Do you pout?
- Do you withdraw from your "offender"?
- Do you give your offender the silent treatment?
- Do you sometimes forget why you got mad in the first place?
- Do you let others' treatment of you affect the way you treat them?
- Do you withhold forgiveness until the one who hurt you apologizes?
- Do little hurts bother you?

- Do you become defensive regarding constructive criticism?
- Do people have to tread lightly around you?
- Do you prefer to think of yourself as a sensitive person?

How do you think we came up with these questions? We are reformed touchy people ourselves. There was a time when neither of us would do very well on a test like this. But by God's grace we are growing in this area, and we are learning as we grow.

Let's take this a bit further. What would you do in the following four scenarios?

1. You are in the car on your way to a business dinner with your husband. His boss and all his coworkers will be there. Your husband turns and looks at you as he is driving and says, "Why did you decide to wear that dress?" Would you:

   a. be hurt and begin to clam up?
   b. chuckle good-naturedly and reply, "Because it reminds me of what I wore on our first date"?
   c. demand to be taken home so you could change into something else?
   d. ask him what he meant by that rude remark?

2. Your husband is observing you as you try to read the small print on the back of a box of cake mix and suggests, "Why don't you stop squinting and put on your glasses? Your forehead is getting a bit wrinkly." Would you:

   a. say, "Good idea; let me try to *find them* without squinting!"—and, with a smile, continue to enjoy his company?
   b. be offended and stop the cake-making process?
   c. retaliate and say something hurtful to him?

3. Your husband watches you preparing an ice cream cone and, recalling that you had mentioned wanting to lose ten pounds, says helpfully, "You're never going to lose weight that way!" Would you:

a. respond by saying that he could stand to lose a few pounds himself?
b. thank him for being supportive in your weight loss program and put the ice cream cone away?
c. glare at him and give him the cold shoulder for the evening?

4. You have just come home from getting your hair cut and highlighted. You notice in the car mirror that your hair is oddly two-toned, very light in the front and very dark in the back. It looks very similar to the way a friend of yours does her hair. Your husband has begged several times, "Please don't ever fix your hair the way Mary does." And now here you are, looking like Mary's twin. Your husband meets you at the door and says, "What have you done to yourself?" Would you:

a. mention that you agree with him and will return to ask the stylist to even out your hair?
b. retreat to your room in tears?
c. get into an argument even though in your heart of hearts you feel the same way?

In each of the scenarios truth was expressed by the husband. Your reaction to truth determines in large measure your husband's freedom to express himself without worry or fear of reprisal.

My (Connie) husband loves to go to movies. I consider most of them a waste of my time and an insult to my pocketbook. I'm usually happy to wait until they show at the Dollar Theater or to rent them at the video store. One night the girls and I had something going on, so Wes took himself to see a newly released science-fiction movie. He had looked forward to seeing it all day. After we returned home that evening, I asked him how it was.

"You wouldn't have understood it," he said.

How hard is it to understand a movie? I thought. *How could he say I wouldn't get it? Of course I'd get it.* "What do you mean?" I asked.

"Oh, you know," he said. "There are a lot of movies you just don't 'get.'"

I thought for just a second about saying, in a tone that was far too polite, "It's not that I don't 'get' them; it's that there's rarely anything to get."

I could tell that I was on the verge of overreacting, so I said nothing. (This is a fairly safe move if you're not sure what kind of reaction is headed out of your mouth, by the way.) I wasn't cold, and I didn't act hurt. I simply closed my mouth for the moment, and then when I opened it, I turned the conversation to other things, thinking I'd mention to him later how his remark had bothered me.

Three days later I had to think hard to even remember what it was about. It didn't seem like that big of a deal anymore, and it wasn't. It seemed kind of funny. There *are* movies I don't get—especially sci-fi ones. I'm still not convinced these movies have a plot, but if they do, they are beyond me.

My husband's intention wasn't to offend me. I knew that then, but I still wanted to let him know I didn't appreciate what he said, and a part of me wanted to pick a fight.

Larry King Live guest Bill Maher, host of *Politically Incorrect,* made a comment recently that was sadly funny but true. He said that there are only two things that give men a reason to lie: The first is to gain and keep political office; the second is to stay married.

What has become more important to you—what you want to hear or the truth? Women who overreact are hard to talk to, and some husbands just stop trying.

In this world where peace is such a rare commodity, it is a wise woman who refuses to take offense over the inconsequential things of life.

Bottom Line: Thick skin is not just for elephants.

chapter fifty-eight

STOP PUNISHING HIS HONESTY

An area in which women build walls but are often unaware of it is in the area of honesty—specifically, their husband's honesty.

Men say what's on their minds. Period. As young girls, women were taught to speak and act in ways that wouldn't hurt someone else's feelings. Surely young boys were taught this, too, but somewhere along the line—perhaps because they're not as relational as we are—young boys turn into young men who have a tendency to speak what's on their minds.

I (Connie) needed a new pair of glasses, so while visiting my parents with our three daughters, I ventured out to shop for frames. With the support of my cheerleading section I chose a trendy shape that perfectly suited my face. My teenage daughters loved the tortoise-colored frames, and so did my mother. How could I go wrong?

When we got back to Omaha, I asked Wes how he liked them. As with everything he does, Wes wanted to give me a well-thought-out, educated opinion. He walked around me, studying my face from various angles. His mind now made up, he said, "I don't."

Taken aback, I told him that his blunt answer hurt my feelings.

"Why?" he asked. "You asked me for my opinion, and I gave it."

"Well," I said, "do you like these better than my old glasses?"

"No, Connie, I've never cared for those either. They remind me of my grandmother." Where was this man's sense of fashion for eyewear? But he is conservative and refined, while I'm more casual and whimsical.

"Now my feelings are really hurt," I told him.

"Connie," he said in his best goal-oriented voice (the goal was to make me think sensibly), "if you don't want my opinion, don't ask. All I'm doing is answering your questions. It isn't a personal insult; we're talking about a pair of glasses!"

My feelings told me we were talking about a lot more than that, but what he said made a lot of sense. Wes hadn't criticized *me;* I just toyed with the idea of taking it that way. Actually, he was only venturing his opinion because *it had been asked for*.

We know of an incidence that occurred several years ago. Two couples that were good friends with one another had gotten together one Friday night for food and fun. After a board game one of the women asked, "If you could choose one quality in a mate, what would you choose?"

First of all, never ask this question to a group of people that is already married! Second, think long and hard before answering the question.

One of the men said with complete spontaneity, "I'd like a wife about whom, when we entered a room together, every man there would think, *Wow, isn't Bob a lucky guy? I wish I had a wife like that.*"

A nervous silence followed his remark, but it lasted only a few seconds. That is because his wife, who was thirty pounds heavier than she'd been on her wedding day, recovered from the shock of what he'd said and proceeded to tell him how shallow he was.

Her husband was taken aback. He couldn't believe he'd hurt her feelings—that was the last thing on his mind. Nor was he saying he didn't love her or that he regretted marrying her, which he didn't. All he was doing was answering the question. He couldn't see why his wife took it so personally. She couldn't see how he could say something like that and believe her feelings wouldn't be hurt.

Another classic case of this is our friend who wanted to find something special to wear to her husband's office party. She searched for days before finding what she thought was just perfect—a silky green pantsuit that seemed especially fitting for the holiday season.

The night of the party she dressed with great care. She waited until her husband had gone downstairs before she donned the new outfit. A few minutes later, she descended the curved staircase. Her husband heard her coming and walked into the foyer. She stopped midway down and said, "Hi, honey. How do I look?"

He took one glance at her and said, "Like Kermit the frog."

She was devastated, and he couldn't understand why.

"I didn't say I didn't like the outfit," he tried to reason with her. "I just said it reminded me a little of Kermit. After all, you asked me what I thought."

Men give their opinions, often freely and without misgivings. They don't think about their remarks hurting you, because if you said the same in return, their feelings wouldn't be hurt. When you can grab hold of this concept, your marriage is on the road to change!

Learn to hear what your husband is saying, and leave it at that. Don't internalize and take personal ownership of every word that comes out of his mouth. Give him the liberty of having an opinion and expressing it, especially if it's in response to a question you or someone else might have asked.

Bottom Line: Embrace the truth, and encourage your husband to speak it.

part five

About the Relationship

keeping the fire going

I'm eighty-five.
I spent the first thirty years of my marriage
expecting my husband to be more like me.
I spent the next thirty years resenting that he wasn't.
Young girls—and that's those of you
under eighty—don't do that.
That's not living; that's drudgery.
You want to live. You don't want to drudge. Trust me.
Understand your man and get on with life.

A FRIEND

Marriage is a bit like a garden. In this section we talk about how to weed, water, and fertilize the garden so that it will blossom and thrive. If you are a gardener then you have discovered, no doubt, that it is pointless to plant flowers that are meant to be in the sun under the porch, where they are devoid of all they need to be sustained. You can poke around at the withering plants, plead with and cajole them, but they absolutely will not blossom. They don't have what they need!

Perhaps that is where your husband is—in a place where he cannot blossom, because he is not getting what he needs. And if that is the case, connecting with you verbally isn't going to be on his mind. What follows are some ideas for tending your marriage garden. We think applying yourself to these areas will not only water, weed, and feed your relationship, but will also help you to change and grow as well.

chapter fifty-nine

LET GO OF HIS HALF

Women often feel that they outgive their husbands in marriage. In the beginning they don't seem to mind, but later on it seems they mind a great deal.

Not long ago we were teaching on the subject of marriage to nearly a hundred women. After a few weeks a woman raised her hand and said, "When is somebody going to teach our husbands how to love us? When will they start doing their share? Why do women give so much more than men?" Many of the women burst into laughter, and a few brave ones even applauded this woman's courage to ask what apparently was on all of their minds.

About this time we were booked to do a radio interview about our first book with a station in Florida. The host of the program was fun and outgoing, and at one point he made the statement that he felt women changed the most after the wedding, while men, in fact, changed very little.

"What are you saying?" we asked. "Are you saying they change for the better or for the worse?"

"Oh, definitely for the worse," he replied.

Feigning outrage, we asked him to explain.

"It seems to me that women are natural givers during the courtship and early marriage years," he said. "We men couldn't outgive them if we tried. But shortly after the wedding, it's as if this small adding machine comes roaring to life, and suddenly a wife begins resenting all the giving she not only chose to do, but also insisted on doing. She holds this over her husband's head until he picks up *her* ball and starts running with it. This poor man has no idea what he's doing with the ball or where he's supposed to run. All he knows is that he'd better run, and run fast. I just don't get it. Women definitely change the most after marriage. We men don't change that much at all."

And after thinking about it, we decided that he was right! Men don't seem to change that much, and this suddenly becomes a problem to wives.

Who gives what to whom? Who changes most? Does it matter? Should you concentrate your efforts on getting your husband to do his part before moving ahead yourself? If you want your husband to talk to you, these are issues worth tackling.

It's not all that unusual or surprising to find a woman investing heavily in her marriage. She's doing what she was created to do, tending the relationship, while the man is doing what he was created to do, tending his work. The happy wife is so eager to nurture and grow the relationship that she may not even notice whether her husband is giving much back in return. *It doesn't really matter—he'll give back soon enough,* she thinks, *as soon as he's had time to adjust.*

Her husband, meanwhile, busily sets about accomplishing his task-oriented goals. He's trying to get ahead at work; he's thinking about the future; and he's thinking about all the things he needs to get done around the house before winter sets in.

As he does this, his wife continues to look for creative ways to let him know she cares. It pleases her to please him, and he readily accepts her warm efforts. He's not aware that she's investing more in the relationship, and she's not either—at least not yet. Remember that she's giving for the pleasure of giving. Since he's not experiencing any pressure to change, he continues on with his tasks, certain that the relationship is on solid ground.

After a while, though, the ground begins to rumble. She begins to notice that things seem rather one-sided, and even household chores take on more weight. *Why do I always have to load and unload the dishwasher? Why doesn't he ever offer to take the trash to the curb? Why do I always organize our social events—even dates together? How can he sit and read the newspaper while the baby screams at his feet? And come to think of it, why do I always pick up his dry cleaning? And, oh, by the way, does he really think I enjoy making seventeen-layer lasagna every time his parents come for a visit?*

At this point, an identity change begins to take place. The woman begins doing less and less—"waiting" for her husband to catch up. She will now only invest in the relationship to the degree that her husband does.

Her husband is probably unaware anything is amiss, at least initially. But over time he can't help but notice his wife's aloofness, and he is sincerely puzzled. Believe it or not, most husbands have no idea that this might have anything to do with them.

This is a critical juncture in a marriage. Many a wife, instead of communicating with her husband how she is feeling, continues to withdraw, waiting for him to get it. She simply can't imagine that her husband doesn't understand how she is feeling, but the truth is that he doesn't. Even when things begin to fall apart, many husbands remain clueless—aware that there is a problem but entirely in the dark about what it might be.

This can be a pattern that lasts for years, and we know from experience that this is a miserable existence. You can choose to live otherwise and continue to work and invest in the relationship, even though it might seem that you are doing all the work.

"What about me? Won't I get lost in all of this if I continue giving regardless of what my husband does?" This is what many women wonder.

It is an excellent question. We've discovered that you don't get lost in the process, that in a sense you find yourself in an entirely new way. You are no longer allowing another's behavior to dictate your own. Your husband may or may not begin to invest more in the relationship, but knowing that you've done what you can to let him know how you feel allows for a peace that wasn't there before.

Our advice is to talk with your husband about how you are feeling before you reach the end of your rope. My (Connie) husband was thrilled when I began to share my thoughts with him. (Well, most of the time he was.) I didn't understand how important this was, and for a number of years I was uncomfortable dealing with negative feelings. I discovered that both of us were much happier when we did.

Sometimes you will just have to let some things go. We have a dear friend who, for over thirty years, has explained to her husband that it would mean the world to her if he would be more affectionate. In fact, she has gone even further by being specific about it, lest he wander around in ambiguity. "If you would hold me for five or ten minutes each night, that would be wonderful," she has explained. Or, "If you would hold my hand sometimes while we're watching a movie, I would feel so loved." She doesn't nag him about it, only mentions from time to time how much it would mean to her.

Her husband, who is an intelligent man, remains unmoved by her requests. This woman is not a whiner, nor is she someone who constantly asks her husband to change. She is gracious and considerate and treats her husband lovingly and respectfully. It would seem that either he doesn't get it or that he doesn't care. The latter is not true, and it would seem that the former isn't either. Simply put, the way he shows love to his wife just doesn't include much affection.

This seems so unfair, doesn't it, especially when she tells him time and again how much it would mean to her? She seems to be asking for so little, and it wouldn't require much from him. After all, she's not asking for the world on a silver platter; she's asking for a little bit of affection. It's so doable! Yet apparently it's not for him.

What's a woman to do? She has two choices. She can either let her husband's resistance embitter her, or she can let it go. After thirty years of hoping for something she has yet to receive, she decided to let it go.

Bottom Line: Your husband doesn't realize how you are feeling unless you tell him.

chapter sixty

DEPART AND REUNITE

Frustrated that her husband wouldn't talk to her, Liz began to shut down. When he walked in the door at the end of the day, she said hello without looking up from whatever she was doing. When he left for work in the morning, she said, "See ya" if she happened to be nearby as he walked out the door. If she wasn't, she made no effort to say good-bye. She felt that she had been the one carrying the burden of conversation in their marriage for over twenty years. She decided it was now his turn.

As the days wore on, it became apparent that he wasn't catching on to her game plan. He made no effort to pick up where she'd left off. She wasn't even sure he noticed that she had stopped carrying the ball, so to speak. Their communication consisted of exchanging information: "What time is Megan's program?" "Don't forget to pick up the dry cleaning." "Do you want to rent a movie tonight?"

How long can we go without having a normal conversation? she wondered. From the look of things, it seemed they might land themselves in the *Guinness Book of World Records* sometime soon.

It was at that point that she enrolled in a class we were leading. The first night she learned about "blastoff" and "reentry." This principle teaches that just as there are two critical phases of launching a rocket ship (blastoff and reentry), so are there two critical times in your home each day.

The first, blastoff, is when you and your husband say good-bye to each other in the mornings. We offered the class several tips they might consider to make blastoff go smoothly. Additionally, we suggested that if there was just one thing each could do to improve her marriage, it would be to walk her husband to the door (or go to her husband if she leaves first), look him in the eyes, hug him warmly, and say, "I love you. Have a wonderful day."

The second phase, reentry, is when a couple reunites at the end of the day. Often the first few minutes they're together sets the tone for the rest of the evening. Again we offered practical suggestions for making reentry a pleasant time.

We encouraged the class to practice blastoff and reentry every day, whether they felt like it or not. "Act now, feel later," we told them.

Liz was skeptical, but she was so weary of the silence engulfing her marriage that she decided to give it a try.

A week later she came to class a few minutes early to tell us about her week.

"I fumbled on the blastoff the first day," she said, "and the rocket sputtered and lurched as it launched. But I did it. The landing was great! He walked through the door as I was stirring something on the stove." She smiled, remembering. "I turned off the burner, set down the spoon, looked into his eyes. (His eyebrows raised in wonder.) Then I smiled. (Now they were beginning to wrinkle.) I hugged him and told him I wanted to hear all about his day. (At this point his eyebrows were deeply furrowed.)

"'What's wrong?' he asked. 'Did something happen today? Did you wreck the car?'

"'No, I didn't wreck the car, and nothing is wrong. I just want to know about your day.'

"He was dumbfounded. Not only had I acknowledged his being home, but I was actually asking about his day. He didn't know what to make of this sudden change. The Queen of the Cold War seemed to be warming, and he couldn't understand it.

"'Did I miss something?' he asked. Surely he wondered if he was in the right house.

"I assured him that he had missed nothing. The car was fine; it wasn't our anniversary; and my mother hadn't called to say she was coming for a three-week visit. 'I simply want to know about your day,' I replied.

"After a few more promptings, he began to tell me. I listened attentively. No one was more surprised at this than me! Not only am I the Queen of the Cold War, I am also the Queen of Interrupting. Rarely does he get a sentence out of his mouth before I jump in and change course. My days always seem so much more colorful! Suddenly I realized how little I had listened to him in the past.

"We sat there for a few minutes as he told me about his day. I found that what might have bored me before actually interested me now. I began to study the dynamics of what was happening. The more interested I appeared, the more he talked. I found this fascinating."

Two weeks later Liz came to class and gave us an update. "I've continued this pattern for several days now. Every night when he comes home, I stop what I am doing and listen as he talks about his day. Each time he talks more and more. Before long he is not only talking about the details of the day, but he is beginning to talk about how he feels and now asks my opinion on things. This is real progress! He's becoming my best friend."

"What was the key?" we asked.

"No question, it was noticing him again and learning to listen to him. That opened the floodgates of communication for us. I discovered that nothing dams them up, at least in my marriage, like being a poor listener."

Bottom Line: If you stop noticing when your husband leaves and returns home, he may stop noticing you.

chapter sixty-one

CONDUCT A HUGGING CLASS

Have you ever noticed that sometimes men just don't know how to hug very well? Hugging can be an easy step to warming up your marriage and familiarizing yourself with each other again.

If your husband isn't much of a hugger, be encouraged—it can be learned!

I (Nancy) have given Ray hugging lessons and talked him through my idea of a hug. Recently, when we were together at the end of the day, I shared something that had upset me. Ray is my staunch defender and immediately got riled up on my behalf. I told him what I needed more than anything was to be hugged. He was more interested in solving the problem, but since hugging seemed to be what I needed, that's what he wanted to do for me.

Ray is a natural born "stiff hugger." As he "stiff hugged" me, I coached him through it: "Relax your arms, darling; go sort of limp. Good! Now stop the vigorous patting of my back, and lean into the embrace." He did, and I began to feel better right away, and told him so. This made him feel wonderful.

"Now say to me very softly, 'Everything will be all right.'" He did. I felt better and better, and so did he.

Even though I had helped him, my body responded to his comforting embrace.

Bottom Line: Hugging is often the kindling that gets the fire glowing.

chapter sixty-two

TAKE OUT THE GARBAGE

As odd as it may seem, garbage—yes, the garbage that you take out to the curb each week—seems to be an Achilles' heel in many marriages. Dozens of women have vented and emoted to us about how their husbands don't take the garbage out in a timely fashion and have asked what should they do about it.

Let me (Connie) illustrate this. It seems silly to me now, but the trash was a sore issue in our marriage for years. Put more correctly, it was a sore issue with me; it didn't register to my dear husband that it was a sore issue unless I reminded him that it was.

Wes simply couldn't remember to take it out on Tuesdays. Every time he forgot, he would apologize and say he would try to remember the next time. And the next time he'd forget unless I reminded him. It was almost easier to just take it out myself, but pride and principle kept me from doing so.

I was frustrated that if I didn't remind him, it didn't get taken out. In the past he had told me he disliked me mothering him, yet it seemed fine that I mothered him regarding the trash; I didn't want to do that. I thought he should be able to remember on his own and that his lapses should be infrequent.

This became something of a part-time job in my life. I was either reminding him that the garbage truck was coming that day, reminding him that it was coming tomorrow, reminding him that I didn't like reminding him, or asking him if we could have a discussion regarding his memory—and all sorts of other things that still make my head spin. The trash seemed to be my crusade.

To avoid this type of frustration in your marriage, we recommend you choose carefully the things you allow to upset you. In my case, it was a simple thing for me to say on Tuesday mornings, "Honey, the garbage truck comes today; would you set it out?" This would not have been hard for me because I always remembered that it was coming.

I timed myself while saying this to him one day. *It took three and a half seconds!* How could this be? For less than four minutes a year, I could save myself a whole lot of frustration. Or I could take it out myself or assign it as a chore to one of the girls. It seems sad to me now that I let such a worthless pursuit frustrate me in my marriage for so long.

Some of you are probably thinking that the point isn't the four minutes a year or who takes out the garbage, but the fact that often a woman serves as her husband's safety net when it seems he should serve as his own.

That's the rub, isn't it? Here's the deal: Someone has to change in this area, so why not let that person be you? Why be frustrated? Simply make an adjustment in those areas. Maybe you don't feel like adjusting, or maybe you feel you're doing more of the adjusting than your husband is. And maybe you are.

But what are your options? You can't choose for him, only for yourself. So why dig in your heels and allow your heart to freeze over while you wait for him to choose differently?

We know that talking about the garbage is just the tip of the iceberg for many of you. There are issues in your marriages that go far deeper than that, and we encourage you to seek help in dealing with those.

What we're addressing here are those daily irritants that can wreak such havoc in a woman's life—the garbage, the toothpaste caps, the dishes on the counter, the cupboard doors left opened, the spills left to dry, a cluttered dining-room table. You get the idea.

Think about it. These are really not that big of a deal, although we often tell ourselves they are. All that is required for smooth waters in most of these cases is that someone adjusts. The problem is that this is not a popular concept in today's culture.

After years of quibbling over this same issue in our own marriages, our best advice is if he doesn't begin taking it out on his own, take it out yourself or adopt the other strategies mentioned earlier. It just isn't worth the time and energy to worry about it, nor should it be a cause of division and strife.

"But he's not doing his part," you may be saying. So what? You're not his mother, and it seems to us that this is the position you place yourself in if you insist on being his conscience on this (or almost any other) issue. If you've asked and asked and asked some more and he still doesn't act, stop asking and do it yourself. As crazy as it may sound to you right now, it may well be that your cheerful servant's heart will motivate him to change more than any words ever could.

Bottom Line: Garbage isn't attractive, especially in a woman's heart.

chapter sixty-three

DISCERN HIS PET PEEVES

Women often wonder why the flow of communication is so stilted in their marriages, yet they don't realize that frequently they are the cause of the stagnation. A woman who isn't skilled at "reading" her husband's conversational pet peeves is shooting herself in the foot. Although we've touched on most of these in other chapters, let's look again at a few of the more common pet peeves and see how you might be inadvertently discouraging your husband from talking.

Men dislike wives' use of the words *always* and *never* so casually and often at their expense, as in, "You never listen to me" or "You always try to solve my problems instead of hearing what I'm saying."

Women talk in general terms—"you always, you never"—but men hear in specific terms. So whatever you say they take literally. That's why they don't take it well when you talk like that, even though it seems like no big deal to you.

When you're dealing with your husband's pet peeves, the temptation will be for you to throw them up at him whenever he breaks his own rules. For instance, when he says "you always," a part of you will want to say, "Tsk, tsk, tsk—you're breaking your own rule."

It is your gentle silence (not your stony or huffy silence) that will allow your man to see the error of his ways for himself, and once he does, your stock will soar in his eyes. What if he lives his entire life without embracing his own rules? God will take care of all of that one day, if you leave room for Him to do so.[1]

Other pet peeves for men include:

- Finishing their sentences.
- Listening with half an ear—even though it may be the very way in which he listens to you.
- Constantly correcting him when he speaks. What does it matter if it was summer instead of fall? Or Tuesday instead of Wednesday? Or that it was Aunt Florence who broke her leg instead of Aunt Hilda?
- Editing his speaking style. "Could have, should have, and would have" are not good phrases to use when you're talking to your husband about his conversational skills. Nor are "Why didn't you just say such and so?" "Is it still today or have you rambled on into tomorrow?" or "Wake me up when you get to the point of the story." This seems so obvious, but frequently women succumb to these phrases in their frustration.
- Asking "What's your point?" or "Where are you going with this?"
- Not leaving well enough alone. In other words, when your husband is talking to you, don't say, "Wow, we're talking more than we ever have before. This is great! Let's figure out what we did to make this happen." Those kinds of things aren't helpful to a man. They are pressure!

Bottom Line: Make it your goal to know what his pet peeves are. Then honor them.

chapter sixty-four

AVOID ARGUMENTS AND ASSUMPTIONS

Do you frequently find yourself arguing with your husband? If you are not careful, arguing can become the only way you converse. It can be such a normal part of your conversational style that to not talk that way would seem strange.

Arguing is a losing proposition. It wears you out, and it's exhausting to your husband. You say words you don't mean, and then you have to live with them. If you argue in front of your kids, you model behavior that's neither becoming nor honorable. Your self-esteem may even drop as you see yourself behaving in such a poor manner. To top it off, rarely is any progress made. The issues that need to be resolved still need to be resolved; only now the issues are heavier and more volatile.

Arguing is like a wrestling match, except that you use verbal blows instead of physical blows. Because women tend to be more verbal, it seems to us that a woman can often "best" a man in these matches and that she may feel a small amount of satisfaction that she can do so.

Most arguments aren't really about who's right and who's wrong. They are about pride and control. It is not the wise woman who argues,[1] for the wise woman keeps herself under control.[2]

You may also find that you have a tendency to resort to arguing if you feel your husband isn't hearing what you are trying to say. When this occurs, we suggest the following:

- Stop talking for a moment, and regain your composure.
- Say to your husband, "I don't mean to argue about this. I'm just not sure you are hearing what I'm trying to say. Can we begin this conversation again?"
- Consider his point of view, and agree with him where you can.
- Ask yourself, "Is this agreement factually based?" "Are we fighting over substance or semantics?" and finally, "Is this really worth arguing about?" Fatigue and/or pride have a way of making small issues loom larger than they are.
- Try restating your thoughts clearly and concisely.
- If he continues to miss your point, try using an illustration. For example: "Remember when you mistakenly thought the deadline for the Frasier project was a week later than it really was? You felt horrible because you still had some work to do on it before it could be presented. Your boss was very understanding and after discussing what had caused the slipup, he didn't mention it again. I think that's how you should handle Ellen's speeding ticket. She made a mistake; she paid the fine and attended classes; and it seems she's learned her lesson. The best thing we can do for her now is the same thing your boss did for you."
- If your husband doesn't see your position after explaining it in a couple of different ways, it may be that he simply disagrees.
- Once the issue is resolved, let him know how much you appreciate his seeing it through to the end. This will encourage him to do the same thing when the next issue arises.

Instead of arguing, some women might resort to whining in this situation. Try to step outside of yourself and listen to your own voice when you are talking. Are you whining? Self-awareness in this area will help you to stop this form of communicating, which is probably very annoying to your spouse.

There may be some things about which you and your husband will never agree. In those cases, you may simply have to agree to disagree.

Try the following when you're in an argumentative mode:

- Train yourself to think about what you're going to say before you say it. If it's contentious or argumentative, rephrase it.
- Ask yourself if you feel the least bit smug in what you are saying. Do you like to make your point and look good while you are doing it? Could it be that you are prone to being argumentative? Train yourself not to speak when you're feeling this way.
- If you find yourself becoming enveloped in an argument, say, "Can we talk about this later" or "Wow, I'm more emotional than I realized about this. Can I have a few minutes to regroup?"
- When you find yourself getting embroiled in the "he yells, I yell louder" cycle, step out of it. A one-sided argument is difficult to carry on for very long.
- When you do stay in an argument to the bitter end, initiate reconciliation. Don't wait for him to come to you—go to him and make things right.

Another problem that can cause arguments is making assumptions. This is what we call a "quicksand" issue—once you make an assumption, it takes mere seconds to find yourself in trouble.

In his book *Coming Home,* James Dobson gives an excellent example of when he and his wife Shirley faced something similar.

> Some years ago I went through a very hectic period of my life professionally. I was a full-time professor in a medical school, but I was also traveling and speaking far more often than

usual. I completely exhausted myself during that time. It was a dumb thing to do, but I had made commitments that I simply had to keep.

Finally on a concluding Friday night the siege was over, and I came dragging home. I had earned a day off, and I planned to kick back and watch a USC-Alabama football game that Saturday. Shirley, on the other hand, also felt that she had paid her dues. For six weeks she had taken care of the kids and run the home. It was entirely reasonable that I spend my Saturday doing things she wanted done around the house. Neither of us was really wrong. Both had a right to feel as we did. But the two ideas were incompatible.

Those assumptions collided about ten o'clock Saturday morning when Shirley asked me to clean the backyard umbrella. I had no intention of doing it.

There was an exchange of harsh words that froze our relationship for three days.[3]

Be a proactive communicator to curtail potential conflict and unpleasant, unexpected surprises.

Bottom Line: Although we could argue all day against arguing, we've chosen instead to say three small words: Don't do it.

chapter sixty-five

DISCOVER HIS PASSIONS

Do you know a no-fail way to get a man to talk? Discover his passions.

A few years ago, my (Connie) husband and I went out to eat with a young couple we had grown to love deeply. Following a wonderful and entertaining meal at a Japanese steakhouse, we went back to our home for dessert.

I had just finished coauthoring *Is There a Moose in Your Marriage?* and Bob asked about it. I quickly summed up how things were going, because the fact is that unless you're a writer yourself, a couple of comments are a couple too many!

Bob, though, continued to ask questions and wanted to see a copy of the book. I told him it hadn't been released yet, so I didn't have one.

"Do you have a draft of some kind I could look at?" he asked. I did and gave it to him. He began flipping through it, and the rest of us began talking about something else. Before long he rejoined our conversation, but when there was another lull, he continued asking questions about the book.

How did we divide up the material? (I don't know. It sort of divided itself.)

How did we find a publisher? (By the grace of God.)

Was it difficult writing with someone else? (No, it was a complete delight.)

Which was the hardest chapter to write? (The one on submission.)

Which was the easiest? (None seemed too easy!)

During what part of the day did I write? (Every part—sometimes at 2 A.M., usually when our girls were in school, rarely late at night, never on weekends.)

Were you relieved when it was finished? (Yes, but I was even more awed at how God had carried us through the process.)

I noticed that he asked questions that *no one* had asked me before—even those closest to me. I also noticed how his eyes sparkled as we talked—his countenance literally seemed to change before our eyes. It slowly dawned on me why he was so interested.

"Bob," I asked, "do you like to write?"

"I love to write," he said. "It's my passion. If I could do anything in the world for a living, I'd write. I've always loved English. I've always loved putting ideas on paper. I've always loved writing, and I hope that one day I'll be able to do that."

His wife nodded in agreement. Then my husband got involved! Although he has no interest in writing, he loves this young man and enjoyed seeing him so enthusiastic. We began to brainstorm how Bob could begin writing in the little free time that he has. Our friend just bubbled over with energy. There was a fire inside him that we were seeing for the first time. Why? Because we had hit upon his passion. We had discovered a vein that ran close to his heart. His wife called later and thanked us for allowing her husband to "dream out loud," as she put it.

"Thank us?" we said. "The pleasure was ours."

To hear another person dream out loud is a unique privilege. Think about it. You are being allowed entrance into a private part of his soul that is rarely exposed. To hear anyone do this is thrilling, but to encourage your husband to do so is a special treasure.

Have you encouraged your husband to dream out loud recently?

Have you studied him and tried to figure out what it is that he really loves to do—not what it is he does for a living, but what it is that makes his eyes light up when he talks?

You may not realize that this is an area of his life that he longs to share with you but may not know how to. It is lying buried somewhere in the depth of his heart collecting dust and cobwebs as he tries to make a life for himself and his family. What a gift it would be for you to help him rediscover it and dust it off.

So few of us ever spend the time to learn what another's passion is, and if we do, it's often with someone besides our spouse. Most likely it's with our children, or with a close friend as we chat over coffee. But with our husbands? Rarely.

I (Connie) hate to admit this, but after our evening with Bob and his wife, I realized it had been years since I'd prompted Wes to dream out loud. I'm cringing as I type these words, even now. Certainly he still has hopes and dreams. Unmet goals and visions. Unconquered territories and unquenched fires. At one time I knew what these were, but they had become fuzzy to me. Life got in the way, children came along, I got busy, time marched on, and passions were shunted aside.

It dawned on me that I didn't want to be eighty-five years old and still thinking that "one of these days" I'd figure out what it was my husband was passionate about! I remembered that it had to do with the ocean, but what exactly? Did he want to study it? Live by it? Sail it? Since I have an aversion to water, I probably subconsciously thought that if I didn't mention it, it would pass. But why would I wish for his passion to pass?

I decided to learn more about it. There was a small part of me that hoped it had nothing to do with me in a scuba diving suit, I must admit. I kind of like getting my oxygen out of the air, not a tank. Nevertheless, I began *that day* to ask my husband questions. What would he do if he could do anything? Where would he live if he could live anywhere? What did he get excited about in life? What was something he always wanted to try but hadn't?

You know what happened? I began to rediscover his passions, as did he. All it took was a little effort, and it was pleasant to do.

Do you know what your husband's passions are? If you don't, ask him! If you do, begin to help and encourage him to realize some of them. If he's always wanted to sail the ocean but you can't afford a boat, order him a subscription to a sailing magazine or rent a sailboat for an hour or two. Drive to the nearest body of water and have a picnic, or take him to a nautically themed restaurant and rent a video with an ocean theme to watch later. The crazier it sounds, the more fun it often is.

Although men are goal oriented, one of their goals may not naturally be to discover what your passions are. It doesn't matter. You can tuck them into the conversation when you are talking about his.

Bottom Line: Passion is what causes the fire to rage in a man's heart. Help your husband's heart rage.

chapter sixty-six

ABOLISH THE COLD TREATMENT

Are you using the cold treatment in your marriage as a means of getting what you want? Do you ever utter the words, "He just doesn't understand"?

Women can be strong, stubborn creatures. As the old saying goes, "We have ways of making you talk." And in this case a woman's way of manipulating her husband is to give him the cold, silent treatment.

This is really hard on a guy. We saw a cartoon recently that showed a man reading about taxes, stress, death, and fire-breathing monsters that were set to invade the earth. He calmly kept reading. Then he turned the page and saw the title, "Cold Treatment from Wives on Increase across the Nation." The previously calm man began to tremble with fear and dread. He broke out in a cold sweat and wanted to run and hide. It was a hysterical cartoon, but it is really not very funny when a wife uses this tactic in her marriage.

You are in effect saying, "Don't talk to me. I am not listening. I don't care what you have to say. In fact, I don't care about you. Period."

Most men—though not all—let go of things much more quickly than women do, and they often have no idea why their wives are upset. How many times have you finally told your husband what's bothering you only to find that he barely remembers what happened? Women think that each degree of coldness serves to "hint" to their husbands what's going on, but it doesn't. They remain as uninformed as ever, wondering why their homes suddenly feel like igloos.

I (Connie) can't tell you how many times in our earlier years I'd resort to this tactic, and later when we discussed things, my husband would say, "I didn't know why you were mad, I just knew you were upset about something."

If you and your husband disagree on something, discuss it freely and openly. Don't think that he will guess why you are upset. Learn to get over things quickly.

Bottom Line: Men don't enjoy living in Virtual, Alaska.

chapter sixty-seven

QUIT KEEPING SCORE

Are you a scorekeeping woman? If you are, your husband is probably not a talkative man. Scorekeeping is not an Olympic event, but too often it's a marital one. Wives who keep score are like computers with no delete button.

Men don't realize that a scoreboard exists and that all too often it runs all the time. Because they're unaware of this, they have no idea that the score is lopsided and that they're perpetually behind.

The scorekeeping wife is just the opposite. She waxes and shines the scoreboard and keeps replacement batteries on hand. She knows what does and doesn't score points, and often she's the one in charge of the ball, too.

Some of the ways in which women keep score include:

- mentally noting when extra time was spent with his family (rather than yours).
- "allowing" him to play golf—or any other activity he does for enjoyment—but then expecting him to "work off his debt" in some other way.

- expecting him to do something he dislikes doing with you because you accompanied him to dinner with his boss, partner, etc.
- counting how much money he spends on himself and making sure you spend the same (or more) on yourself.
- doing a number of errands for him and now expecting him to do the same for you, or do extra things around the house because you feel he's indebted to you.

I (Connie) remember once discussing the "score" with my husband. He didn't realize we were discussing it because he didn't know about scores. I quickly ran through the list of things I was disgruntled about, and I'll never forget him saying, "Wow, Connie, it's as if you're keeping score or something."

Of course I was, and he was behind!

By the grace of God both of us are now retired from scorekeeping, and you can be as well. Our advice is to put away the scoreboard in your marriage. We had a good friend who did this. After only a week of score-free living, her husband asked suspiciously, "What's going on? You're different. For the first time in years, I feel like I can just be me. I don't feel like you're trying to turn me into someone else. It doesn't seem like you're always mad or exasperated like you used to be. You seem...you seem...well, you seem as though you like me again. What are you doing? I can't put my finger on it, but this is a whole new you, and the newer version is much more pleasant than the old one."

What the woman had done was set a torch to her scorekeeping ways. Ironically, as she told us later, it was when she put away the scoreboard that her husband had the freedom to become the man God intended him to be—because all his energies weren't spent trying to stay out of trouble with his wife.

Bottom Line: Leave scorekeeping to the referees.

chapter sixty-eight

DON'T GO THERE!

Sometimes keeping control of our actions requires all the strength we can possibly muster. The question we are addressing here is: How do you react to your husband's moods, his edginess, his tone of voice, his quarrelsomeness?[1]

Yesterday, my (Nancy) husband returned home from a four-day trip. He arrived shortly before I got home from work. I had stopped at the store to get supplies for a welcome home dinner. I tooted the horn as I drove into the garage, which is at the back of our home. He saw me from the kitchen window. As I parked the car and was beginning to wrestle with the groceries, I saw him hurrying toward me. *How sweet!* I thought, abandoning the groceries to embrace him. He half-heartedly gave me a hug and queried, "Where did you put the mail? I've been looking for it."

I told him where it was, and then he asked, as I was coming into the house, "Where are my glasses?" Since he must have had them on his trip, I was clueless about their present whereabouts. He began to look for them, mumbling a bit to himself—something like "I can't believe this. I just had them in the car!" We both looked in the car with no success.

He then related that he'd had a late lunch, and suggested that instead of having the dinner I'd brought home, why didn't we have something else—something I didn't have the ingredients for. Next he shared with me how tired he was after driving over four hundred miles, and wasn't it a little hot in the house?

Well, it was certainly getting that way!

With the first hour behind us, he decided to go upstairs and change clothes and unpack. I walked over to the kitchen window, took several deep breaths (read: letting off steam) and said aloud to myself, "Don't go there!"

I (Connie) had a similar experience. It occurred the very week we were wrapping up this book. You'd think that since I've studied and surveyed and researched and written on this topic for the past several months I'd be equipped to handle almost anything! But not on this night.

My youngest daughter was playing in a piano concert downtown, which Wes and I planned to attend with her. Our twin older daughters had plans to meet some friends at a local restaurant. It was mid-November, and snow was beginning to fall as we headed downtown. By the time we got there the roads were extremely slick. Just as we arrived at the concert hall, a four-wheel-drive vehicle turned the corner and spun out of control right in front of us. All I could think about were our twin daughters, who have only had their licenses for about six months. They were already at the restaurant and probably had no idea how slick the roads were. I wanted them to leave the restaurant immediately and get home before the roads became any worse.

I ran into the concert hall and asked to use a phone as Wes and our daughter went on in. I called the restaurant and was told that the group my girls were with had just left. I was extremely worried. There was nothing else I could do, as they didn't have a phone with them. I said a quick prayer, went into the hall, and sat down by Wes.

Although I am normally fairly stoic, I was near tears. I told Wes how upset I was and spent the next few minutes telling him why. I told him that I didn't even feel very well, either. My stomach had been upset all day, I said, and now it felt like it was going to rumble right out of my body. I finished my monologue and waited for him to respond.

After making certain I was finished, he picked up the sports page, which he'd brought in with him from the car, and began reading it.

You know what I wanted to do at this point? I wanted to *go there.* How on earth could he sit so calmly? But remember: Men don't worry, fret, or fuss. Plus, I was doing enough of that for the both of us.

So I took a deep breath and mentally went to the "kitchen window" as Nancy had, telling myself the same thing: *"Don't go there."* Even though that's exactly where I wanted to go, I knew that *there* was a pointless place to visit—even briefly.

There is taking the wrong fork in the relationship road. We've both spent a lot of time traveling down that fork. And we can tell you that it is a dead-end street. *There* represents several major choices women often make, and none of them leads to the restoration of loving conversation with your husband.

So often women choose to retaliate; this choice initially seems so appealing that we can hardly resist. How easy it is to join the "game" in progress. When a tired man serves the conversational ball, it is tempting to return a few down-the-line winners, or perhaps ace him outright. All of us are responsible for our actions, but just because one of us is in a mood doesn't mean the other has to join in the "fun."

A gentle response to a man's short temper will defuse it, whereas a tit-for-tat response kindles both of your tempers.[2] Kind words heal and help.[3]

It is helpful if you don't subconsciously record the things that annoy you. And it is a fortunate man who is married to a woman who doesn't record grievances against her husband and who settles things quickly without bringing them up again.

Remember erasing the board when you were in elementary

school? All the writing disappeared in a flurry of white dust. The next day the board was fresh again for new things to learn. Can you imagine how hard it would be to learn if year after year everything written on the blackboard was still there? It would be impossible!

Bottom Line: Learn to stop and go to the "kitchen window" rather than "there."

chapter sixty-nine

THE SKINNY ON NAGGING

Don't you just hate the very sound of the word *nag?* It brings to mind an old horse that basically serves no purpose. You can begin to see the tie-in, though, when you consider that nagging serves no purpose whatsoever in a marriage.

Often what women see as helpful advice men see as nagging. This never ceases to amaze us! But it can quickly become one of the hot spots in your marriage if you're not careful.

Men don't like to be reminded of things over and over, nor do they want our advice unless it's asked for. Interestingly, we've discovered it can be especially difficult for a man to take advice from his wife. This makes no sense to a woman, because who would have his interest at heart better than her?

Recently a man we greatly admire spoke to a large audience. "You know," he said, "the fact is that it's just plain hard for a man to take advice from his wife unless he asks for it. He can take it from others, but it takes an especially confident guy to take advice from his wife." Some things in life are just hard to understand, and this is one of them.

Not too long ago Ray and I were on our way to Nashville, Tennessee, to visit one of our children. Ray is tall and long-legged and therefore always requests the exit row on the plane. The exit row has more legroom, and it is also the place where the emergency door is located, which has a complex series of instructions displayed on it. Every time we sit there, I study this guide. Ray, however, never looks at the guide. In exercising my civic responsibility I have asked him a time or two if maybe he shouldn't check the instructions, since the lives of many passengers could potentially be in his hands.

On this particular trip, Ray reminded me in his shoot-from-the-hip conversational style that I had asked him this very question a hundred times, and would I mind not asking again. Dealing with verbal outbursts about my helpfulness has never been my strongest suit, and I had to make a quick decision: Would this vacation be full of fun, or would the silent treatment be a better choice?

Is nagging or even offering unasked-for advice an issue in your life? We've learned that many men find it especially difficult to take helpful suggestions from their wives; yet we have such wealth to share with them! Unless he asks, though, save the wealth for another time.

Bottom Line: The difference between helping and nagging is usually a matter of whether or not your opinion was sought out by your husband.

chapter seventy

DON'T EMBARRASS YOUR HUSBAND

Your husband will be more apt to speak to you if he can count on you not to embarrass him publicly or privately—especially publicly. Men are not as thick skinned or as macho as we sometimes think, and they don't like being embarrassed, especially by their wives.

Often these conversations start out with "You'll never believe what Tom did" or "Tom did something that was so funny—you're going to love it." By the time the wife has finished her story all eyes are on Tom, who is awkwardly shuffling about. Women will often laugh, as they don't want to hurt the feelings of their friend who is telling the story, but there may be a nervousness to their laughter; they don't want to hurt Tom, either. Some of the men won't be laughing because they know too well how Tom feels and that it's not good.

I (Connie) used to tell a story about the first time my husband took me skiing. This usually came up when someone would start talking about different personalities, and those of us with type A spouses would start giving examples of things that had taken place in our marriages.

My story would often take the cake: We were newly engaged, and I had never skied before. Wes loves the sport and is a fantastic skier.

He overestimated my abilities (*way* overestimated them), and on my second day out he had me on the black slopes. On the mogul hill. Of the steepest mountain. Telling me to hurry. For you nonskiers, this is like asking your two-year-old to run the Boston marathon. And win.

Because I was madly in love with my husband-to-be and didn't want to disappoint him, I slipped and slid and screamed and catapulted down the hill. I never once said, "I'm scared," "I don't want to do blacks yet," "I prefer my legs unbroken," or "I'll wait in the lodge with my cocoa." I somehow thought my love for him was connected with whether or not I could ski the black slopes.

By the time I finished my story people would be laughing hysterically. They especially liked the part where he raced to the bottom and looked back up to see me quaking in my boots, still at the top of the mountain. I told how he motioned impatiently for me to hurry up so we could get to the next run without wasting precious ski time. It *was* kind of funny.

Somewhere along the line, though, I noticed that Wes stopped laughing and just sort of endured my story. I was having fun at his expense. I never added how he had changed over the years and would never do this now; that he hated it more than anyone that he did it then; that his actions were simply a result of his youth and immaturity—that would have been the honorable thing to do. I didn't know to do it then because of my own youth and immaturity. We both exhibited youthfulness and immaturity—Wes on the ski slopes and me by telling the story. Wes just didn't expose mine like I did his.

Don't embarrass your husband, no matter how funny your stories are. Don't laugh at his expense. Don't make him fodder for others, either. He can tell the stories if he wants to, but he needs to know that these stories won't come from your mouth.

Bottom Line: Stay off the black slopes.

chapter seventy-one

WHEN YOUR WARRIOR IS TIRED

When we were beginning to write this book, I (Connie) asked my husband how he perceived love. I was expecting a fun repartee of thoughts and ideas. *This could be one of our best discussions ever,* I told myself. *I bet I'll learn a lot about him I didn't know before.* I could hardly wait to hear what he had to say.

He, however, had just come in from working an extra-long day in which he'd been on his feet for most of the time. He looked at me as if I'd just dropped in from another planet and then replied, "I don't perceive love when I'm tired." Period. In other words, *Leave me alone for now—I'm too tired to think about it!*

I have just witnessed the shortest repartee in history, I thought. My conversation starter had lasted exactly seven seconds—one second shy of how long rodeo riders are required to stay atop a bucking bronco.

It can be a wild ride trying to get your husband to talk to you, especially when he's tired.

When a woman is tired, she still perceives love—much more so than a man. He wants to be left alone and given time to unwind. He doesn't want to have to deal with anything.

She may feel the same way, but not as deeply. In other words, she's not as single tasked about it as a man is. Loving overtures toward her are welcomed with open arms. They make her feel better and less tired. A man may not receive them as gladly or as openly. It's not that he doesn't want them; he's just too tired to appreciate them at that moment. However, the more tired a woman is, the more she'll appreciate another's efforts to make her feel better.

Besides exhaustion, timing is a critical element, too. Many men don't like to talk just as they get home from work (Wes doesn't; I knew that but still hit him with a major question the moment he walked in the door. That was not a smart move on my part, to say the least).

If something is bothering them or they are preoccupied, men won't want to engage in conversation and will prefer to be left alone. After a warm welcome, be willing to give your husband some space when he comes home from work or is preoccupied. Each person is different, of course, so study your husband and determine what makes him open up and close up.

Remember that men show love differently and that just because he doesn't feel like talking when you do, it doesn't mean he loves you any less.

After the shortest repartee in history, my (Connie) husband picked up the mail and flipped through it. There was a life-insurance bill in the mix. "This is how I show love," he said, tossing me the envelope, "even when I'm tired."

Romantic? Not particularly. Flowers and candy? Nope. Sweet nothings whispered in my ear? Rarely. But does he show love? You bet. Even when he's tired. Just as your husband does. Sometimes we just need fresh eyes to see it for what it is.

Bottom Line: When your warrior is tired, let him rest. You can talk later.

chapter seventy-two

LEARN TO NAVIGATE STORMY WATERS

One of the most challenging times to try to get your husband to talk to you is when the storms of life hit. These could include job loss, physical injury, death of a loved one, depression, marital discord, or a host of other things.

The dynamics of communication, which are often fragile because of our differences, become even more fragile during stormy times. When these occur, it's important to know what to expect from your husband, because he'll behave far differently than you would under the same circumstances. You may be his only calming force and your steadfast love and support may be what carries him through. Though not always, you may find that your relationship with your husband is actually enhanced as you travel through the storms together.

One of the biggest differences between men and women during these times of upheaval is in how they react. The first thing men generally do is withdraw. This is foreign to a woman's way of thinking; it's the last thing she's inclined to do. Her first instinct is to circle the wagons and gather around. Call in support! Get the word out! When the storms of life roll in, women go into overdrive. They make phone calls, rally the troops, and line up meals. By nightfall a storm-tossed woman is surrounded by friends, family, chocolate chip cookies, and casseroles.

Men, though, prefer to be alone. *This is one of the rare times in life when women are the doers and men are the be-ers.*

I (Connie) remember not too long ago when my husband seemed extremely quiet and removed. He said very little at the dinner table and listened politely when the girls or I said something, but I noticed that there just wasn't much input from him on anything. He was withdrawn. As I thought about it, I realized he'd been that way for the past several days. You would have thought I would notice it sooner, but I didn't—life has a way of doing that sometimes.

That evening after the girls had left the table I said to him, "You seem kind of quiet, honey. Is there anything you want to talk about?"

He said, "No, I guess not." When a man uses the word *guess* in this context, that is usually a great clue that things are not okay. I didn't push the matter, but instead told him that I thought he was a wonderful guy and that if he was feeling burdened about anything, I was there to listen if he ever wanted to talk.

We went on to discuss other things, but a few minutes later he returned to our former conversation. He spoke of an issue that had occurred recently that had bothered him greatly. He was as devastated as I'd ever seen him. We talked the situation over and discussed how he could best handle it. He seemed to feel better about it afterwards. Had I not noticed his quietness and remarked on it, though, I don't know if he would have mentioned it.

Men like to protect their wives from worries and concerns, and your husband may not openly share these issues with you. Your discernment in noticing his quietness or other signs that indicate he's bothered may well be what encourages him to talk. Don't insist that he share with you if you sense something is wrong or if he alludes to the fact that there is. Insisting will only make him more withdrawn. If he wants to share, he'll share when he's ready. Your part is to let him know you're there for him.

Wes and I began to weather the storm together. A few weeks later my husband said that if there was any silver lining in the black cloud of this situation, it was that it brought us closer together. All I could do was give praise to God, for there were times in our marriage in years past when if my husband was withdrawn, I didn't respond as I did at that time.

If your husband seems more withdrawn than usual, tell him you love him and ask if there is anything he'd like to talk about. Don't keep asking, though. Simply let him know that you're there for him, and then be there for him.

It's important to study your husband and know what ministers specifically to him during life's stormy times. For some men it's simply being left alone. Others like knowing that their wives are nearby. One woman we know canceled many of her outside appointments just to be near her husband. There was very little talking unless he initiated it, which he rarely did. Yet her presence meant the world to him, as she found out later.

Often it is the nonverbal I love yous that speak loudest to a man. This can be a hard concept to grasp because so much of what we do and how we love is verbal. Whenever we tell a friend we're hurting, the first thing she does is throw her arms around us, and say, "Oh, I'm so sorry this is happening! Let's talk this through and figure out what to do about it." Regardless of whether or not the problem is solved, talking seems to make both parties feel better.

Your husband, though, probably won't be like this. His energy levels are at an all-time low—don't expect him to utilize what little energy he has left in conversation with you. What you'll end up doing is causing him to withdraw even more. When this happens, the dynamics really get jumbled, because often a woman will take this added withdrawal as personal rejection and become upset and hurt herself. Resist the urge to take things personally during stormy weather. Your husband doesn't need a poor relationship with you on top of what he's already trying to deal with. When your husband is ready to talk, he'll start talking.

We have a friend who took her two-year-old son to the doctor because he wasn't talking yet. After examining the boy, the doctor said to the mother, "Relax, Mom. When Max is ready to talk, he'll talk. Stop fretting about it and enjoy him." Those are words worth heeding.

What do you do when a man withdraws? We suggest the following:

1. Don't express disapproval, condemnation, or feelings of rejection.
2. Don't beg him to talk to you.
3. Give him plenty of space—*warm* space! Too often when men withdraw, women respond with the "cold" treatment. Men don't need this when they're withdrawn and hurting.
4. Don't offer solutions unless you're asked. It doesn't matter if you have the perfect solution. Wait until he asks your opinion before sharing it with him.
5. Don't get depressed yourself because he's withdrawn.
6. Don't obsess over his withdrawal.
7. Keep things in perspective. This will help keep your own attitude right.
8. Be there for him.
9. Let him know, by doing and saying small things, that you're thinking about him: a note, a special meal, a backrub, buying him a newspaper or magazine he doesn't normally read, or suggesting that you both do something he enjoys.
10. Pray for him—this is the best remedy of all.

When one or both of you is grieving over a situation, keep in mind that men and women often grieve differently. A man's grieving time is often shorter than a woman's and is usually more specific.

When tragedy strikes, your marriage can become especially vulnerable to division and conflict. Statistics show that many marriages break up under such strain. Although your grieving will probably be different, you can help each other through it by understanding each other's needs during those times and by providing for them as best you can.

The storms of life can bring a couple closer than ever if handled with generous amounts of love and sensitivity and with a forgiving heart.

Bottom Line: Be extra sensitive to your husband and his ways when storm clouds hover.

chapter seventy-three

MAKING IT TO THE OTHER SIDE

Men prefer being alone when stormy weather hits, which is often why they seem to lag in their support of us during our stormy times. They often have no idea what it is we want or need, so they simply do what is natural for them—they do unto others as they would have done unto them.

Don't look for your husband to circle the wagons when you're hurting. This is not a part of his emotional DNA makeup. In fact, he may not even be around. He may be off golfing or watching a movie. This is because he's assuming that you want time and space to think things through. He's giving you what he would want.

A dear friend of ours recently lost her mother. Weeks went by, and her deep grief continued. One day her husband said to her, "What is wrong with you? You seem upset all the time. You're no fun to be around anymore."

Our friend burst into tears. Between sobs she told him how desperately she missed her mother and how she couldn't seem to overcome her grief. Her husband was shocked. Speechless. Completely taken aback. He had no idea that her distant mood had anything to do with her mother's passing—after all, she had died the previous winter, and summer was now in full bloom.

Men react differently than we do. Their period of grief is shorter, and they're able to detach more easily from sad situations. Once their grieving is done it's usually done. It's doesn't float in and out of their lives like it does ours. Occasionally something might make them think of their loved one, but it won't bring back the flood of memories it does for us. Men grieve and get on with their lives. Women tend to make grieving a part of their lives long after the loss occurs.

Don't punish your husband for grieving differently than you do or for not understanding your grief. One of the biggest steps you can take toward getting your husband to talk to you is to stop thinking that your responses are "right," and that his are "wrong." When you're grieving, the best thing you can do for your husband is tell him exactly what you need, no matter how elementary it seems:

- "I need you to hold me right now. Don't talk and don't ask questions. Just hold me."
- "I'd like to tell you how we used to celebrate Mom's birthday. It would mean a lot to me if you'd listen."
- "I'm feeling so sad today. I feel like crying. It has nothing at all to do with you. I'm still grieving for my dad. Would you take a walk with me later?"
- "I know I'm irritable right now. I'm sorry. I've been thinking about my friend in the hospital, and it's really gotten to me."
- "I feel afraid and sad. I need you to put your arms around me and tell me everything will be okay."

When your husband does these things for you, thank him and express your appreciation. This will make him feel great. He loves meeting your needs, especially when you feel wounded or blue. He just doesn't always know what they are or how to meet them.

Bottom Line: When the shoe is on the other foot and you're grieving, don't expect chocolate chip cookies, casseroles, or deep conversation unless you ask for them. And even then, realize that the request may have gotten scrambled in the translation.

chapter seventy-four

DON'T MAKE HIM A "PROJECT"

One of the fastest ways to have the conversation ebb more than flow in a marriage is to make your husband into your project. Whether you're trying to change the way he eats, dresses, fathers, or mows the lawn, no man enjoys being his wife's project, regardless of her good intentions.

One woman asked her husband what she did that irritated him most. His answer: "When you make me your project. No matter how nonchalant or discreet you think you're being, I can tell when you're doing it, and I hate it."

That's called telling it like it is, and that's how most men feel.

Making your husband your project says to him that he's not good enough as he is. It makes him feel mothered, managed, and demeaned.

I (Connie) remember doing this with my husband. My project was his behavior in social situations. He is more of an introvert, while I am more of an extrovert. As a result, he interacts with new people differently than I do.

I decided that with my help he could change. I didn't ask him whether he desired my help or whether he wanted to change. But I began coaching him as to what he should and shouldn't do when he was first introduced to someone.

It didn't take long for him to figure out what I was doing. In fact, one evening on the way home he asked me to stop—right in the middle of one of my coaching seminars. I was disappointed, for my arsenal of good suggestions had barely been tapped. But he wanted no more of them. So I stopped. From then on he did great on his own, and we both enjoyed ourselves far more without my constant surveillance.

Interestingly, several years later a couple of incidents occurred that made me wonder if he'd be open to a few well-intentioned suggestions. Since he no longer felt like my project, I thought he might be receptive.

One morning I said quite simply, "Honey, if you would ever be interested in a few tips about conversing with someone you've just met, I have a couple. But I want you to know one thing: My intention isn't to get you to change. I like you just the way you are."

"I'm not interested," he said immediately.

Who could blame him? Why would he volunteer for the starring role in *The Return of Project Man* after what he'd been through in the past?

"Okay, honey, that's fine," I said, and I dropped the issue.

Later that night after we'd eaten dinner, he said out of the blue, "Okay, tell me one thing."

"What are you talking about?" I asked. I had totally forgotten about our conversation.

"You can tell me one thing—and just one thing—about what you mentioned earlier."

So I gave him a quick tip right off the top of my head, and he gladly received it.

"That's easy enough," he said. "I can see how that would help."

As we talked, I started to suggest a second thing he could do.

"No, I just asked for one," he reminded me. "I don't want any more."

I laughed and told him that old habits die hard, and then *I stopped talking*. He has yet to ask for any additional tips, which is fine.

If a man feels like a project, not only will he not ask for your input, but he also won't receive it even when it is for his own good.

Bottom Line: If you want a project, take up knitting.

chapter seventy-five

DON'T EXPECT HIM TO MEET ALL YOUR NEEDS

One thing we noticed as we researched this topic is that time and again women expect their husbands to meet a huge majority of their needs, but that their husbands are often unable to do this.

Two possible explanations come to mind:

1. Men are underachievers in this area.
2. Women are overly expectant.

Although many of you could make a great case for explanation number one, let's instead look at number two. If you can begin to effect change in that area, you may find changes occurring in number one as well.

Men have no desire to fill 100 percent of our socialization needs. Or even 80 or 70 percent. We asked our husbands what they thought about this. They both suggested that between 35 and 50 percent would be plenty—on a very good day, they added!

I (Connie) was fortunate to be raised in a loving home, yet I don't recall my dad talking endlessly to my mother. We lived on a farm, and in addition to farming my dad also worked full time as a firefighter at a nearby military base. He was a busy, hardworking man. Often, after finishing the day's chores, he would play softball out in the front yard with my sisters and me until it became too dark to see. My mother cheered us on from the steps of the front porch. These are still some of my fondest memories of growing up.

As I look back, I see that my mother displayed a great deal of wisdom in not expecting my dad to meet all of her emotional needs. She maintained other friendships through church, family, and a local women's club. The bulk of her talking was done with these women, which let my father off of the hook in a big way. He wasn't her only outlet of sharing and didn't have to come up with umpteen thousand words at the end of the day to meet that need.

Of course they still talked, but she didn't pressure him to talk more than he was willing to. As the years went by she discovered that he talked more and more. The financial and emotional pressures of raising a family lessened as each of us left home, and the firm foundation they had built over the years became even firmer.

Just a few months ago I was visiting them in Oklahoma, and as I stepped out of the shower early one morning I heard my mother laughing gleefully. I assumed she was on the phone with a friend. A few moments later I realized my dad was telling her something humorous that had happened to him the day before. He found in her a warm, receptive audience. *This is one of life's greatest luxuries,* I thought, *to hear one's parents laughing together like this after fifty years of marriage.*

Studies show that when women have even one close friend, their marriages are healthier than those of women who don't. Why? Because of the inordinate pressure that is taken off a husband and the benefit that occurs from talking to another woman.

If you're feeling lonely and have no friends, take the first step toward making one. Someone once said that the only way to have a friend is to be one. Take the initiative and call someone up for lunch or a walk. Volunteer at your local library or hospital. Sign up for a class that interests you. Get involved. If you have young kids, call another mom who might be feeling the same way, and pick a time each week to get together and do something. You may well find yourself energized by these new relationships, which will give you and your husband something new to talk about!

Bottom Line: A close friend is a tonic for the heart, not to mention the marriage.

chapter seventy-six

LAUGH!

One vital ingredient of a happy marriage is laughter. In the relationship between a husband and wife, extraordinary sweetness develops when there is a sense of fun and playfulness. There are exchanged glances and private jokes instead of icy glares and verbal jabs. Smiles abound and cheerfulness is the norm. Sound appealing? It is! And you can begin to implement this in your marriage.

A woman who looks at life with humor can actually become a medicinal agent for her husband.[1] Humor can be developed, and should be, because it actually contributes to good health.

Laughter's known benefits include:

- It stimulates the immune system.
- It pulls together various parts of the brain rather than activating a component in only one area. Perhaps this is one reason that people often find that a dose of lengthy laughter can be followed by a burst of creativity and *problem solving*.
- It's a good cardiothoracic workout. It increases the activity of the heart and stimulates circulation. After laughter subsides, the cardiovascular system goes into a state of relaxation.

- It raises the threshold of pain. It has been shown that five minutes of giggling may provide up to two hours of pain relief.
- It reduces stress.
- It stabilizes moods.
- It rests the brain.
- It enhances communication.

Bob Dole, former U.S. Senator and past presidential candidate, relates that one-liner quips often broke the tension at tough Senate negotiations. He had learned this skill when he worked at a soda fountain. He noticed that the more quips and one-liners he used with the customers, the longer they stayed, the more they bought, and the bigger the tips were. Years later, recovering from the wounds of war, he noted the essential healing agent humor provided for those veterans who were healing after surgery, pain, and months of hospitalization.

In a less dramatic but equally essential way, one-liners can often defuse the grumpiest husband.

Traveling fifteen hundred miles with four grade-school children in a station wagon for a week can try the patience of any man, and Ray was no exception. On this particular journey we were taking the children to Williamsburg, Virginia—probably at my urging, since it was such a historical city. I had been once before with my parents. Ray felt that since I had been there, I should know the town very well. He was trying to find the heart of the city, with no luck. He had an aversion to maps, so we didn't have one. He was making one wrong turn after another. The children were growing weary, and the driver's nerves were getting edgier and edgier.

Finally he announced to one and all, "We will just keep driving until your mother recognizes something!"

I then said something like—"I no longer recognize anything, not even the driver! Who are you? What have you done with my husband?" Ray laughed until tears began to roll down his cheeks.

What I felt like saying was, "You are lost! Get a map! Let me out of this car! This is no fun!" That kind of reaction, I have learned the hard way, escalates tension. We had enough of that in that car already.

There is a time for everything, and a season for every activity under heaven,...a time to heal,... a time to build,...a time to laugh.[2] Wouldn't it be wonderful if we learned how to heal, build, and laugh at some of the situations that confound us?

In an episode of the sitcom *Archie Bunker,* Edith was speaking to her daughter, Gloria. Gloria was upset with her husband, and Edith was counseling her. She told her about an argument that had changed the lives of her parents, which had transpired over pancakes. She said, "Gloria, you can't break up a marriage over something as trivial as pancakes!"

Life is filled with problems and struggles, but when viewed through the prism of faith, we see they are opportunities for personal growth. We don't have to go through life making small issues the reasons for hot debates, when a lighthearted answer keeps the home an enjoyable place to be.

What would happen in our homes if we were slow to speak and slow to anger?[3] Language is the expression of thought. Every time you speak, your mind is on parade. Is your parade a joy to be around?

The real test of this is when our husbands say something about us personally. We would do very well to develop a sense of humor about ourselves. Barbara Bush, wife of the former president, possesses a sense of fun that made her one of our most popular first ladies. She once told a writer for *Ladies' Home Journal,* who was asking her about her famous faux pearls and gray hair, "There is a myth around that I don't dress well. I dress very well—I just don't look so good." Now that is a parade that makes us smile!

Another president's wife once left the White House early one morning to visit a prison in Baltimore, slipping away without waking her husband. When she called to tell him that she was at the prison, he replied, "I'm not surprised, but what for?" Surely they both laughed and enjoyed that moment together!

Here are some practical tips to help you reintroduce laughter into your home:

- Use endearing names, even funny ones, from time to time. After my (Connie) husband helped our twins with their physics homework one evening, I called him Albert (Einstein) for the rest of the night.
- Be affectionate. It seems to us that frequent laughter is often one of the side benefits of affection and that in fact, affection seems to invite laughter.
- Tell a silly joke, and laugh at *his* jokes. My (Connie) husband loves to laugh at one of my jokes that is particularly simple. (These are the only kind I can remember!) He doesn't laugh because he thinks it's funny; he laughs because he loves knowing that I enjoy hearing him laugh at my jokes. If things get a bit too serious, I'll ask if he wants to hear my knock-knock joke about the impatient cow. That said cow has lifted dozens of dark clouds looming on the domestic horizon.
- Meet somewhere totally off the wall or out of the norm. Go to a drive-in and order a root beer float or a cherry limeade.
- Cultivate friends that know how to enjoy life. Laughter is infectious.
- Hold his hand when he's telling you something amusing. Look into his eyes as if he's the only person on earth (there is no law against this).
- If he tells the same joke over and over again, laugh over and over again. It does something to a man when his wife laughs with him rather than rolling her eyes and heaving a derisive sigh. I (Connie) had an aunt that would often reach over and place her hand over her husband's when he was telling a joke, smiling as he spoke. She did this at other times, too—she just wanted to touch him. He was a bit gruff and undemonstrative, to say the least, and never did this in return, but she didn't care. She was wise enough to know that life was too short to wait on him for something he might never do.
- Make dates, and keep them. So often these are the first things to go on our calendars.

- Don't bring up serious subjects on a date. Hold that thought for another time. If your husband does, say, "Let's talk about that later and just have fun tonight." There was a time in one of our lives when I went on a date with my husband and insisted on hashing out an extremely controversial issue. When the date was over and my weary husband rose to leave, he remarked, "I *never* want to sit at this table again when we come here in the future." It was that "unfun" of a night.
- Have a place where you can go and laugh together—a laughter table, in a sense.
- Don't laugh at your husband—laugh *with* him. There's a big difference.
- Make an effort to do one fun thing every day for your husband.
- Lighten up. Keep things in perspective.
- Laugh for the pure joy of laughing. Laugh again. And again. And again.

Don't you think it's time we added *laughter* to our to-do list? Then everyone could begin their day with an activated immune system, a stronger heart, increased brain activity, and a stronger sense of connection with her husband.

Bottom Line: Laughter is the exclamation point of life!

chapter seventy-seven

HUMILITY? ARE YOU KIDDING?

This brings us to another trait that is sometimes served up rarely in marriage: humility. Ouch, ouch, ouch, and double ouch—is that what you're thinking? Then read on.

You know what humility is? Of course you do. Therefore we are not going to recite Webster on this one. But apart from its technical definition, humility is giving up the right to be right. And that can be a hard thing to do. Especially in marriage. When you're nearly always right. Right?

Are you still with us? Have you slammed the book shut and thrown it out? We hope not. Humility is one of the ingredients that can turn not only your marriage around, but your life as well. It will open doors that you never realized existed. It can start you moving down the timeline of your life in fast-forward motion—so quickly that it can sometimes take your breath away. And it's the best heart softener that we know of.

Humility can defuse a situation almost instantly. I remember a time when I (Connie) asked my husband a simple question about something. He was tired and answered me rather sharply.

You know what I wanted to do? I wanted to take offense. And I did. Just as soon as the sharp words had escaped my mouth, he got a phone call that lasted for a long while. By then I had gone to bed and fallen asleep. We think it's wise counsel to not let the sun go down on your wrath,[1] and I didn't intend to—but in this case it was too late, the phone call was too long, and my eyelids were too heavy.

Early the next morning I was spending some time with the Lord, and of course I was instantly convicted about my huffy attitude from the night before. So as soon as my husband woke up, I went to him, threw my arms around him, and said, "Honey, I am so sorry about my attitude last night."

"That's okay," he said. "I forgive you."

Actually I was sort of expecting my apology to prompt one of his own; after all, he was the one who had become irritable first, wasn't he? I thought he might say some *slightly* altered version of the following: "Oh, my wonderful, precious, adorable wife, I know you were simply reacting to *my* irritability, and I take full responsibility for yours! You aren't to blame at all. I'm the one who needs to ask your forgiveness. Will you please forgive me? I am so sorry. You are so thoughtful to be the one to apologize first, even though—let me say it again—it was my fault."

But you see, this didn't happen. He graciously accepted my apology and went on about his day.

And you know what I did? I went on about mine—feelings unruffled and neck veins unpopped.

This is a big change from years past, when I would have rehashed the incident to remind him exactly who said what, when. But you see, it doesn't matter. What matters is that my relationship with my husband flourishes. And what matters even more than that is that my relationship with God does as well.

Certainly there may be cases of emotional or physical abuse where of course it matters greatly. If you are in that situation, seek help immediately. We're talking, though, about the daily routines of life that have such a way of setting us off. Those things that make us draw a line in the sand and say, "You're wrong, I'm right, and I'm going to mount a full-scale war until you acknowledge these facts. And if you think I'm chilly now, just wait. You ain't seen nothin' yet."

Later that morning I called my husband at work. I just wanted to let him know that I loved him. There were times in our marriage when that was the last thing I felt like doing, and it's by the sheer grace of God that those times are behind us. So I called him and told him I loved him. I didn't realize that he was on the speakerphone and everyone in the office next to his could hear what I was saying.

Do you know how thankful I was that I had learned to let things go and wasn't calling him to give him a piece of my mind regarding my interpretation of the previous night's events? The people in the adjoining room would have heard a completely different person saying completely different things. It wouldn't have been a pleasant thing to hear. And most of all it would have reflected poorly on the one I call Lord.

Humility is one of the biggest steps out of the marital dungeon, and it keeps you living like a king and queen. It is often the spark that reignites dormant conversation and is a pleasure to be around.

Humility? Are you kidding? Not at all.

Bottom Line: Humility: Money can't buy it, and department stores don't carry it. It's free. It's fabulous. And it beautifies from the inside out.

chapter seventy-eight

CONSIDER BECOMING A SERVANT

Why is it that we are awed by the services Mother Teresa performed for the hopeless and helpless in Calcutta? Why is it that we marvel as we see the dedication of missionaries on the field in various countries? Why is it that we are thrilled when we see a dog being rescued from a perilous perch in a flood and commend those who helped in the effort?

Why then, do we roll our eyes and laugh in disbelief when we hear of a wife who simply brings a cup of coffee to the man she married who is still sleeping in bed? Are great acts of service better than small acts of servanthood? It seems to us that one of the side effects of service is an open door to interaction.

Mark Twain once noted that kindness was the language that the deaf could hear and the blind could see. Who doesn't want to talk to a person who is kind?

Recently we were having a brainstorming session with our editor, who had flown in from Chicago for a whirlwind three-day session with us. We were discussing various formats, and each of us seemed to be on a different page. We decided to take a break, and I (Nancy) asked who wanted a cold glass of club soda. Everyone did. I then asked if they would like to have frozen peach slices in their glasses instead of ice cubes. Yes! They were delighted with the result and oohed and ahhed over the chilly peaches hovering in the stemmed glassware. They thanked me profusely for serving them like this.

We commented that if we shared this story with other women, they would have agreed. But, we wondered, what would the reaction have been if we said that we did this for one of our husbands?

It has become almost politically incorrect to do such niceties for one's husband. It's cool to serve your kids, friends, acquaintances, and even complete strangers, but not your husband. Why is that? Since when have pleasantries, manners, graciousness, and random acts of kindness toward husbands gone out of style?

We know of a woman who had made all the arrangements to visit her sister for a well-deserved rest. Before she left, her husband had a crisis come up in his business. He was so undone about this that he couldn't think of a course of action to take. She canceled her plans, became his sounding board, and together they thought of a solution that worked. She helped him in every way. He was so grateful that he called her father and tearfully commended his outstanding daughter. They had been married for nearly twenty-five years. Because of her generosity, she is experiencing a fresh outpouring of his love, deeper than it has ever been. Her husband trusts her[1] and she is his delight. He loves talking to her and about her. He called me (Nancy) not too long ago just to share how wonderful she is. I agreed with him 100 percent. His wife is my only sister and sole sibling, and I have learned much from her example. She has yet to make another trip to see me, but she said she wouldn't have missed the journey she took with her husband for anything in the world.

When you serve, there is no guarantee that you'll be served in return. And often, perhaps almost always, you won't be. But we're not here to be served; we're here to serve.[2]

Now that's countercultural thinking, isn't it? Our postmodern world loves countercultural thinking, but not that kind. Who on earth would want to be a servant—where does that get you?

It can get you to places you will never go otherwise, that's where it can get you.

Do you consider servanthood beneath you, especially in regard to your husband? Is a grateful response necessary for you to continue serving him? What if that response never comes—are you going to stop?

What motivates you to serve? Would you be more enthusiastic about serving a king? If an inheritance were involved, would you be a bit more eager? And what if this inheritance weren't just anybody's but God's? Whoa! Surely that would get your attention. On top of all that, what if you learned that this inheritance was not only valuable in this lifetime, but for all eternity as well? You'd be ready to sign on the dotted line, wouldn't you?

Well, guess what? It's all true. God says that whatever we do, we're to work at it with all our hearts, as working unto Him, not men. Because it's Him we ultimately serve. He goes on to say that when we do this, there's a reward, and it's an inheritance from Him.[3] That's right, God! You can stack up all the wealthy estates in the world, and they wouldn't amount to even half a grain compared to this royal one.

Thinking in these terms sort of puts a different spin on things, doesn't it? As well it should. There's something about wanting to please God that changes a person.

The motivation of kindness, deserved or undeserved, may be what causes your husband to begin communicating with you. But what if he doesn't? You continue on as unto God Himself. One day you will receive a reward, and it will make it all worthwhile.

God notices what you do. He notices all that you do. He notices when it seems that no one else does.

What is He seeing in your life?

Bottom Line: Is servanthood a stranger in your home? If it is, reintroduce it.

EPILOGUE

The woman looked up at the emergency physician. "Please, do something," she begged as her husband lay motionless beside her. "Please help my husband."

The doctor looked sadly into the woman's face. In her early eighties, she was the picture of love and devotion as she pleaded with him to intervene on her husband's behalf, although she was undoubtedly scared and shaken herself.

"I'm sorry," he said tenderly, "but your husband is dead. There is nothing we can do. His heart attack killed him instantly."

"No, he can't be dead," the woman insisted. "Please try again. Try anything. *Please*. He can't be dead."

"I am so sorry," the doctor repeated gently, "but there's nothing more that can be done."

She refused to be moved by his words and continued to ask the impossible. "There must be something. Please. Try anything. Anything. Please, Doctor. I'm begging you. Help my husband."

The doctor took the woman's hands as he choked back his own tears—touched by the depth of love that he saw in this dear woman's heart.

"Ma'am, I would give anything in the world to help your husband. But he's gone. I am so sorry."

Finally, his words began to sink in. Her husband was dead. How could that be? Just minutes earlier they'd been having a wonderful conversation, another typical night in their lives. They had been so happy together.

She turned away from the doctor and gently laid her head on her husband's chest. As she did, it moved. "Look, Doctor," she said urgently, "his chest moved. He's not dead! He's alive! Did you see it move? I know that it did—I felt it. Do something! Please. There's a chance he can make it. Please help him live."

The doctor could barely speak. If only he could do what she so desperately wanted. But he couldn't. He once again took the woman's hands in his own and explained to her that the weight of her head on her husband's chest had caused it to depress, nothing else. The monitor had long been flat, and all that could be done had been done.

"I am so sorry," the doctor said yet another time, taking away the woman's last hope.

At last she understood that this was final—that there would be no last-second resuscitation, no paddles brought out to shock her husband's heart into pumping again, no modern-day miracle. Her husband's time on this earth was over.

She turned to her husband, who was lying on the table. She looked into his work-worn face. She lovingly stroked the cheek on which she had planted countless kisses for so many years. Her tears fell as she gazed into the closed eyes.

The doctor's own tears ran freely as he witnessed this tender one-sided exchange. He listened as the woman whispered to her beloved sweetheart, "You were such a good husband to me. You loved me so much, and I thank you."

The doctor realized that he was witnessing one of the great love stories of all time. In his twenty years of emergency work, he had never seen devotion of such magnitude expressed. It appeared from their outward dress that these were humble people who had known hard times. But it was obvious that they had shared a life of enormous wealth because of what they carried for each other in their hearts.

The woman had had no time to prepare for this moment. She had not rehearsed what she'd say under such circumstances. Amidst the ventilator and crash cart and monitors and IVs, the woman spoke what was on her heart—with no audience to hear her, no one to impress.

You were such a good husband to me. You loved me so much, and I thank you.

Isn't this the way you want to love your husband? Don't you want to reach the end of your life, look back, and know you gave it your all?

There is something that happens to a woman who chooses to love her husband as unto the Lord. One of the things is that when she comes to her life's end, she'll look back at this area with no regrets.

Don't you want to be a no-regrets kind of woman? Don't you want to lead a no-regrets kind of life...kind of marriage? Isn't this the example you want to model for your children?

You can begin to live that way today by loving your husband as he is now. Or you can wait for him to change. To think more like you. To respond more like you. To be more like you. To jump through the hoops you've determined that he needs to jump through before you will give him your seal of acceptance.

Be a woman who loved rather than one who waited! To do that, all you have to do is begin. And then you have to keep on. And keep on keeping on.

The only way to do this is by the power of God, for your own power will run out—as it always does. But you know something? His never does. Your tank may be empty, but He can fill it up—as many times as you need Him to.

Your husband may never talk to you the way you'd like. What matters is that you do your part. One day you'll answer to the Lord for how you lived your life, just as your husband will.

There is someone who *will* talk to you, and someone who will listen as well. There is someone who will love you unconditionally and give you the love and acceptance you long for. That someone is the

Lord Jesus Christ. He's the One who can give you the power to live a no-regrets kind of life. Our prayer is that you'll live such a life with Him by your side.

Thank you for reading our book! We wish you much joy and happiness and lots of warm communication in your marriage. Most of all, though, we wish for you a life that brings honor and glory to God.

The publisher and author would love to hear your comments about this book. *Please contact us at:*
www.multnomah.net/husbandtalk

NOTES

CHAPTER 1

1. Genesis 2:15, 18

CHAPTER 2

1. Matthew 6:25, 27

CHAPTER 3

1. Gary Smalley and John Trent, *The Two Sides of Love: Using Personality Strengths to Greatly Improve Your Relationships* (Wheaton, Ill.: Tyndale, 1980), 35.

CHAPTER 5

1. Gary Chapman, *The Five Love Languages* (Chicago: Northfield Publishing, 1992, 1995).

CHAPTER 12

1. Patrick M. Morley, *What Husbands Wish Their Wives Knew about Men* (Grand Rapids, Mich.: Zondervan, 1998), 222–3.

2. Luke 6:35, NASB

CHAPTER 13

1. In the creation account given in Genesis, God formed man of dust from the ground, and breathed into his nostrils the breath of life;

and he became a living being (Genesis 2:8). God placed him in a garden He had planted in Eden (Genesis 2:9), and told him to tend, *guard* and keep it (Genesis 2:15, AMP). Besides tending the garden, it was Adam's responsibility to protect and oversee those in the garden. His charge was to keep those in the garden from danger by watchful attention.

CHAPTER 15

1. Ephesians 5:33, TLB
2. John 3:16
3. Colossians 1:10

CHAPTER 16

1. Genesis 2:24

CHAPTER 18

1. John Gottman, *Why Marriages Succeed or Fail* (New York: Simon and Schuster, 1994), 29.
2. Proverbs 11:25

CHAPTER 19

1. I made a personal commitment to Christ in 1981. I had been invited to Bible Study Fellowship, taught by Anne Graham Lotz, daughter of Billy Graham. She clearly gave out the gospel message. She revealed that:

- God loved me and wanted me to experience His peace and life. "For God so loved the world that He gave His only begotten Son, that whosoever believeth in Him should not perish, but have everlasting life" (John 3:16, KJV).
- Being at peace with God is not automatic because by nature I was separated from God. "For all have sinned and fall short of the glory of God" (Romans 3:23, NIV).

- God's love bridges the gap of separation between God and me. When Jesus Christ died on the cross and rose from the grave, He paid the penalty for my sins. "He personally carried the load of our sins in His own body when He died on the cross" (1 Peter 2:24, TLB).
- I could cross the bridge into God's family when I received Christ by personal invitation. "But as many as received Him, to them He gave the right to become children of God, even to those who believe in His name" (John 1:12, NASB).

To receive Christ I needed to do four things:

1. ADMIT my spiritual need. "I am a sinner."
2. REPENT and be willing to turn from my sin.
3. BELIEVE that Jesus died for me on the cross.
4. RECEIVE, through prayer, Jesus Christ into my heart and life.

I prayed a prayer that contains these thoughts, and so can you. *Dear Lord Jesus, I know I am a sinner. I believe that You died for my sins. Right now, I turn from my sins and open the door of my heart and life. I receive You as my personal Lord and Savior. Thank You for now saving me. In Jesus' name I pray, amen.*

CHAPTER 20

1. Proverbs 15:30

CHAPTER 21

1. Patrick M. Morley, *What Wives Wish Their Husbands Knew about Men* (Grand Rapids, Mich.: Zondervan, 1998), 50.

CHAPTER 23

1. Matthew 18:18–33; Luke 6:38
2. Colossians 3:13

CHAPTER 24

1. Frank B. Minirth and Paul D. Meier, *Happiness Is a Choice* (Grand Rapids, Mich.: Baker Book House, 1978), 174.

2. Ibid., 197.

CHAPTER 25

1. Matthew 19:8–9

CHAPTER 26

1. Proverbs 20:6, paraphrased

2. Proverbs 31:11

3. Luke 16:10

4. Jeremiah 12:5

CHAPTER 27

1. Matthew 7:7–11

2. Mathew 6:25–34; Isaiah 41:10

3. Genesis 2:18

4. John 15:10, paraphrased, "If you keep My Word you will abide in My love."

5. John 15:12

6. John 15:4–5; Philippians 4:13

CHAPTER 28

1. 1 Corinthians 7:4

CHAPTER 31

1. 1 Corinthians 7:5

CHAPTER 32

1. Jean Lush, with Patricia H. Rutherford, *Emotional Phases of a Woman's Life* (Grand Rapids, Mich.: Revell, 1987), 23–4.

2. Ibid., 1.

CHAPTER 33

1. Proverbs 17:22

CHAPTER 37

1. Remember Eve in the Garden of Eden? She was in a perfect setting, in a perfect world, with a perfect husband. And God Himself was with them. She and Adam could have anything they desired, except to eat from a certain tree. This worked well until a sly-talking serpent entered her world and convinced her to do things her own way. And women have been doing the same thing ever since (Genesis 3:1–7).

CHAPTER 41

1. 1 Peter 3:1–2
2. 1 Corinthians 13

CHAPTER 45

1. Some men may use silence as retaliation for hurt feelings. If this is the case, you may be able to break this cycle by remaining friendly and cheerful and continuing to treat him in a loving way. See Luke 6:27–36 for what Jesus has to say about such treatment of those who are treating others unfairly.
2. Matthew 6:25–34

CHAPTER 52

1. Proverbs 22:11
2. Proverbs 11:25
3. James 3:5–6

CHAPTER 55

1. 1 Corinthians 13:5

CHAPTER 63

1. Proverbs 24:17–18

CHAPTER 64

1. Proverbs 20:3

2. Proverbs 29:11

3. James C. Dobson, Ph.D., *Coming Home* (Wheaton, Ill.: Tyndale, 1998), 66–7.

CHAPTER 68

1. We are not talking about abuse. Abuse is a very serious matter, and you need to seek help if this is occurring.

2. Proverbs 15:1

3. Proverbs 15:4

CHAPTER 76

1. Proverbs 17:22

2. Ecclesiastes 3

3. James 1:19

CHAPTER 77

1. Ephesians 4:26

CHAPTER 78

1. Proverbs 31:11–12

2. Matthew 20:20–25

3. Colossians 3:23–24

STUDY QUESTIONS

part one: About Him
why can't He Be More Like Me?

Chapter 1 Men Express Love by Doing

As you go through the questions for chapter 1, be mindful that all that transpired happened before sin entered the world.

1. What do you notice about the difference in the ways that Adam and Eve were created (Genesis 2:7, 22)?
2. Why do you think that God created man and woman at separate times?
3. In what ways were they the same (Genesis 1:27)?
4. What does it mean that man and woman are created in the image of God?
5. How were they different in the *tasks* they were given (Genesis 2:15, 18)?
6. What do you see significant in the task Adam was given, in relation to the nature of man and his inclination to be a "doer"? How then might a man show love to his wife?
7. How were their tasks also similar (Genesis 1:26, 28)?

Chapter 2 Men Don't Worry, Fret, or Fuss

1. In your marriage, who would you say does more of the fretting and fussing?
2. Why might this be? Do you think men care less? Do you think women care more?
3. How should you handle anxiety (Matthew 6:25–34)? How do you handle anxiety?

Chapter 3 His Personality Is Different from Yours

1. From the profile in this chapter, what is your personality type and what is your husband's?
2. Can you think of people from the Bible who have your husband's personality type? Do you think your type is better than his?
3. Would you say that one problem in marriage today is that a woman tends to hold her husband's personality against him?
4. Would your husband say that you do that to him? How can you rethink this issue?

Chapter 4 Men Love Solutions

1. Knowing that most men are problem solvers, how can you adapt yourself to receive advice from your husband?

Chapter 5 You Speak Diverse Love Languages

1. What is your husband's love language?
2. How can you make your husband feel loved today? This week?
3. Have you ever verbally shared your love language with your husband?
4. How willing are you to love him if he doesn't reciprocate (John 13:34–35)?
5. What do those verses say about a person who loves as God loves her?
6. What does Jesus say about loving a difficult person (Luke 6:27–38; Romans 12:17–21)?

Chapter 6 Men Don't Listen the Way Women Do

1. How does this information help you to understand your husband's listening capacity?
2. If your husband doesn't enjoy lengthy conversations, how have you adjusted/not adjusted to this fact?

Chapter 7 He Needs Processing Time

1. How can you adjust in a practical manner to the way your husband processes information?
2. If an adjustment is necessary, how can you begin to change the way you present an issue that needs processing time?
3. How did Mary and Joseph process differently the news that she would be the mother of Jesus (Matthew 1:18–25; Luke 1:26–38, 46–55)? How were their reactions the same?

Chapter 8 What's Obvious to You Isn't Obvious to Him

1. How well does your husband know where he stands with you?
2. Do you think he should read the "signs" you are giving him, such as remoteness, sighing, a lack of responsiveness, being quieter than usual (Proverbs 10:9; Psalm 15:1–2)?
3. Who do you think is responsible for your happiness?
4. Where does true joy come from (John 15:11; Galatians 6:22–23)?

Chapter 9 Men Stick to Single Tasks

1. If this is true of your husband, do you hold it against him? What can you do to change your reaction?
2. How many things can you do at once?

Chapter 10 He Isn't Like You Spiritually or Emotionally

1. Your husband has been gifted uniquely by God with natural abilities. As he matures, he also acquires skills, and if he is a

Christian, God gives him spiritual gifts. What natural abilities has He given your husband?

2. What skills has he acquired since you met him?
3. What do you think his spiritual gifts are (1 Corinthians 12; Ephesians 4:11–13)?
4. Would you say you spend more time focusing on his strengths or on his weaknesses? If you spend more time thinking about his weaknesses, how does this affect him? You? Your relationship?
5. Have you thanked God for your husband's unique personality (Psalm 139:13–16)?

Chapter 11 Men Don't Use Details the Way Women Do

1. How might God be using the small issues of life to train *you* in patience (Colossians 1:10–12)?

Chapter 12 Men Go through Seasons

1. Does God give people "second chances" (2 Chronicles 33:1–13)?
2. Do you think this king deserved a second chance? Why do you think God did this for him?
3. How does Jesus respond to a woman who needed more than a second chance (John 4:7–27)?
4. What did she do as a result of having a second chance (John 4:28–30)?
5. What could you do to help your husband reconnect with you, even if he has not yet reached out to you?

Chapter 13 You Married a Warrior

1. Do you hold your husband's maleness against him? In what ways?
2. In what ways could you let your husband know that you celebrate his manhood?

3. Have you thanked God for the wonderful differences between males and females (Genesis 1:27)?

Chapter 14 Nothin' Says Lovin' Like Somethin' from the Oven

Although we realize that every day may not include a family breakfast or dinner together, we believe that some effort should be made to reestablish the tradition of dining as a family.

1. What are your mealtimes like (Proverbs 31:14–15)?
2. What priority does meal preparation have on your to-do list?
3. When was the last time you fixed your husband's favorite meal?
4. What are his favorites?
5. If good nutrition is important to him, how do you help him in this area?
6. How often do you eat together as a family?
7. Would you say your children's activities take priority over family meals and/or family time together? If so, how does your husband feel about this?

Part Two: More about Him
Different Strokes for Different Folks

Chapter 15 Spell R-e-s-p-e-c-t His Way

1. Why should a woman see to it that she respects her husband (Ephesians 5:33)?
2. What does *respect* mean to you?
3. What are some things a wife might do to show her husband that she respects him?
4. Suppose a woman doesn't think her husband deserves respect. What should she do?
5. What might be the result if a woman simply gives respect to her husband because she knows God wants her to?
6. How might this impact her relationship with her husband?

7. What influence might this have on the children in the family?
8. How might a child's respect for his or her father be affected if his or her mother doesn't treat Dad with respect?
9. How might the family dynamics be affected by the wife's choice to respect her husband?

Chapter 16 Accept Him

1. Why do you think a man needs to feel accepted by his wife?
2. Why is it important for a wife to accept her husband (Romans 15:7)?
3. What is the ultimate outcome of accepting your husband (Romans 15:7)?
4. Whose example are you following when you accept your husband the way he is?
5. What were you thinking when, during your wedding ceremony, you said, "I take *you*...."?
6. When you said, "I take you for better or for worse, for richer or for poorer, in sickness and in health...", what did you have in mind?
7. How do you think it affects a man when he no longer feels accepted by his wife?
8. How do you differentiate between your husband's behavior and who he is as a person?
9. When there is a problem between the two of you, how do you express it?
10. Do you feel accepted by God (Psalm 139; Hebrews 2:5–8; John 3:16–21)?

Chapter 17 Embrace the Power of Appreciation

1. In what ways might a wife express her appreciation to her husband in everyday life?
2. What do you think would be the result if your husband felt appreciated?
3. What do you appreciate about your husband?

4. How long has it been since you have expressed appreciation to him for something specific?
5. How might appreciating him affect you (1 Thessalonians 5:18)?

Chapter 18 Begin to Say Thank You

1. What priority do you place on behaving in a gracious manner with your husband (Ephesians 4:29–32)?
2. What importance does Christ place on the way you treat your husband (Matthew 25:31–40)?
3. Why are your behavior and the words you use so important (Mark 4:13–20)?
4. When was the last time you thanked him for taking care of the family by working?

Chapter 19 Men Love to Be Admired

1. Does your husband have to "fish" for compliments?
2. Why do you think it is important for *you* to admire him?
3. What did you admire about your husband before you got married?
4. What about his character and physique do you admire today?
5. When was the last time you thought to verbalize your admiration of him?

Chapter 20 Smile!

1. What is the typical look on your face when you are around your husband?
2. What does a cheerful face produce (Proverbs 15:30, TLB)?
3. What produces a joyful appearance (Genesis 4:6–7; Proverbs 31:10–31, [see v25])?

Chapter 21 Put the Wind Back in His Sails

1. Why should a wife encourage her husband (1 Thessalonians 5:11; Hebrews 3:13; 10:25)?
2. In what ways could you encourage your husband?
3. What do you think the results of encouragement might be?
4. How did the encouragement of Barnabas affect his listeners (Acts 11:22–26)?
5. Are you a Barnabas in your husband's life?

Chapter 22 Your Husband Needs to Be Needed

1. Why did you marry your husband?
2. How can you make your husband aware that he is an important part of your life?
3. What can you do to show him that you need him?
4. Name some things he does for you that you cannot do for yourself.

Chapter 23 Silence the Marriage Silencer

1. Are you a forgiving person?
2. What happens when you do not forgive (Matthew 6:8–15; 18:18–35; Luke 6:36–38; Romans 12:17–21)?
3. Instead of forgiveness, what kind of behavior do women (and men) sometimes demonstrate against the offender?
4. What does forgiveness mean to you?
5. What happens to you if you don't forgive on a daily basis (Ephesians 4:26–27)?
6. If you struggle with anger and unforgivingness, what can you do (Philippians 4:13)?

Chapter 24 Choose to Forgive

1. Do you live by your feelings or by your will?
2. How is one able to forgive (John 15:1–5)?

3. How can you apply the six steps to forgiveness given in this chapter?
4. What is the result of forgiveness?
5. Have you asked God to forgive you (1 John 1:5–10)?
6. Have you forgiven yourself?

Chapter 25 Keep the Past in the Past

1. Are you a woman who keeps a list of past wrongs?
2. What does the Bible say about love and letting go of past offenses (1 Corinthians 13:5)?
3. When you have a disagreement with your husband, do you bring up past grievances?

NOTE: If infidelity or abuse is an issue, you must forgive but you must also seek pastoral counseling.

Chapter 26 Be Loyal

1. How loyal are you to your husband?
2. How safe are his name and reputation in your hands (Proverbs 31:10–12)?
3. When your husband confides in you, can he trust you completely to keep the matter private?

Chapter 27 Become His Cheerleader

1. Who cheered you on as a child, and how did that encourage you?
2. What do you think the result would be if you became your husband's personal cheerleading squad (James 5:13)?
3. How do you think it feels to a husband never to be cheered on by his wife?
4. Where does a woman get the strength to cheer her husband on, when she is struggling herself (Philippians 4:10–13)?

part three: About You I Didn't Know That!

Chapters 28–31 Tend the Garden, Come-ons, Lovemaking, Housekeeping

1. Does your husband feel frustrated sexually? (This question is not for sharing with others.)
2. How important is this aspect of your relationship to you? To him? (This question is not for sharing with others.)
3. When was sex first introduced (Genesis 1:27–28; 2:22–25)?
4. Who introduced sex to the husband/wife relationship?
5. When is it right to deprive your husband of sex (1 Corinthians 7:3–5)? What might happen if you deprive your husband of sex (1 Corinthians 7:5)?
6. Read 1 Samuel 1:19. Notice when Elkanah lay with Hannah. Are you only available to your husband during certain times of the day?
7. What does the Word of God say about the authority of the body in the marriage relationship (1 Corinthians 7:4)?

Chapter 32 Get a Grip on Your Hormones

1. How do you deal with the cycles in your life?
2. How would your husband say you deal with them?
3. What are some practical things you might do to remain on an even keel during the times of the month that are difficult for you?
4. List any other suggestions you have found to be helpful.

Chapter 33 Your Unhappiness Affects Your Mate

1. What has helped you to overcome unhappiness in the past?
2. How might changing the way you talk to yourself help you in this area?
3. How can you take your mind off of yourself (Colossians 3:14)?
4. What difference can the Word of Christ dwelling in you make (Colossians 3:12–17)?

Chapter 34 What Do I Do with These Feelings?

1. What governs your behavior more, your feelings or your will?
2. How can you get your feelings to line up with your will (Philippians 1:27)?
3. Can you do this on your own (John 15:5)?
4. How, then, can you love an unlovable person?
5. Do you believe that if you conduct yourself in a way the Bible says to be right, your feelings will catch up to your behavior? Have you ever tried this?
6. What does Jesus say is the result of obedience (John 15:9–14)?
7. Can a woman be taught how to love (Titus 2:4)?
8. What should love "look like" in a marriage (1 Corinthians 13)?
9. If your love doesn't look like this, what can you do?

Chapter 35 Recognize Familial Patter

1. Does your family of origin have a way of talking to each other that is different from the way your husband's family communicates?
2. In what ways have you been holding this against him?
3. How have you made your husband feel about the manner in which he talks to you?
4. Does he talk to you in the same way he talks to his family?
5. Has your husband told you that he finds you difficult to talk to? Why might that be?
6. How do you respond to the truth?

Chapter 36 Don't Play the Semantics Game

1. Do you play the semantics game?
2. How should you speak (Proverbs 8:6–9; 23:16)?
3. What danger in speaking are we all prone to (James 3)?

Chapter 37 Control the Urge to Control

1. Would your husband say that you are a controlling person?
2. What is the underlying issue for a "controller"?
3. How did Sarah try to control a situation in her marriage (Genesis 16:1–2)? What were the results (Genesis 16:3–5; 21:8–20)?
4. When does it seem that control became an issue (Genesis 3:6, 16)?
5. If you have been a controller, what can you do to change?

Chapter 38 Stop Mothering Him

1. How might a woman "mother" her husband? How do you think a "mothered" man feels?

Chapter 39 Get Your Priorities Right

1. Where does your husband rank on your list of priorities?
2. Where would he say he ranks? Ahead of the children?
3. After God, who should have top priority in your life (Genesis 2:24)?
4. What effect do you think it has on a marriage if a woman doesn't place her husband first on her list?
5. How can a woman reprioritize her list?
6. What did Jesus say about Martha's priorities (Luke 10:41–52)?
7. What do you think a man's response would be to being first (after God) in his wife's affections?

Chapter 40 Quit Feeding the Monkeys

1. When your husband helps you, do you criticize the way he does it?
2. How set in your ways are you?
3. Would your husband say you put your standards on his attempts to help you?
4. How quick are you to applaud his smallest efforts?
5. If criticism has become a way of life, why should you change (Matthew 7:1–5)?

Chapter 41 Introduce Mystique

1. How might a wife bring freshness to her relationship with her husband (Song of Solomon 7:10–12)?
2. How might time away together reinvigorate your relationship?
3. What would surprise and please your husband?
4. Would you say that your relationship is in a rut? What would he say? What could you do to change that?

part four: About the Two of You
Lighting the Coals of Communication

Chapter 42 Learn the ABC's of Listening

1. Have you ever thought of listening as an acquired skill?
2. Describe a good listener.
3. How would you grade yourself on a scale of 1–10 as a listener (10 being excellent)?
4. Why do you think it is rare to find a good listener?
5. What did you learn in this chapter that was new to you?
6. What happens to a wise person who listens (Proverbs 1:5–6; 4:1)?

Chapter 43 Avoid Listening Pitfalls

1. After observing the examples in this chapter, what kind of listener are you?

Chapter 44 Develop Great Responses

1. When your husband talks to you, do you respond to what he says?
2. What suggestions in this chapter have you put into practice, and what were the results?

Chapter 45 Listen to His Silence

1. How do you handle your husband's silence?

Chapter 46 Lighten His Load

1. How often do you extend a helping hand to your husband?
2. Why should you (Genesis 2:18)?
3. If a man perceives love through acts of service, how might an offer of help minister to him?

Chapter 47 Use Mars Protocol

1. What is the easiest way to get your husband's attention?
2. How can you tell that your husband is really listening to you?
3. Of the nine points given in this chapter, which were the most helpful to you?

Chapter 48 Don't Expect Him to Read Your Mind

1. Why might your husband more easily understand the direct approach?
2. When was the last time your husband could tell what was on your mind simply by looking at you?

Chapter 49 How to Ask for Help

1. What has been your approach in asking for your husband's help?
2. What specific things do you need help with?
3. How quickly do you expect him to do something?
4. Would it be practical to give him some lead time to follow up on your request?
5. If you have children, what is expected of them regarding helping you?

Chapter 50 "If I Have to Ask, It Doesn't Count"

1. Which of the five points in this chapter seemed most helpful to you?

Chapter 51 If at First You Don't Succeed

1. How patient are you with your husband? How willing are you to restate the same request with kindness (Proverbs 15:18; 16:32; 19:11; 25:15)?
2. Why do you think God allows your patience to be tested (2 Corinthians 6:3–10)?

Chapter 52 Frame Your Words

1. When was the last time you critiqued yourself to discover how you speak to others?
2. There are several ways in which the truth can be communicated. Have you made an effort to speak in a gracious manner that edifies the listener (Proverbs 22:11)?
3. Have you noticed a difference in the manner in which you speak to your friends, your children, your husband? What is it?

Chapter 53 Paint Your Words

1. When was the last time you used a word picture to describe how you were feeling? What was his reaction?

2. How did Jesus often speak (Luke 11:33–36)? What is your response to this kind of teaching?

Chapter 54 "Am I Still Your Darling?"

1. In what new ways can you say something so that it isn't a turn-off to your husband?
2. Since code phrases trigger playfulness and intimacy between a couple, a project for this week is to monitor your present response to his silence, mood, and his reaction to what you are *presently* saying or doing. What needs to change? (We're talking about *you!*)

Chapter 55 Announcements Don't Work

1. What is your husband's reaction to announcements? Do they turn him off? What better ways can you think of to get his attention?
2. What is your response to announcements? How do they make you feel?

Chapter 56 Don't Go On and On

1. What is your expectation *of* your husband when you talk to him about a problem?
2. If you want him to simply be a sounding board, do you mention that?
3. What is his expectation of you when he tells you about a problem?

Chapter 57 and 58 Develop Thicker Skin/
Stop Punishing His Honesty

1. What is your response to the truth (Proverbs 8:7–11)?
2. If what your husband tells you is true but hurts your feelings, how do you handle it (Philippians 4:8)?

3. Is your husband afraid to tell you what he thinks because of your anticipated reaction (James 1:19)?
4. What does that reveal about *you* (James 1:20)?
5. How should you receive what your husband says to you (James 1:19)?

NOTE: The number one reason the men in our survey gave for not wanting to talk to their wives: a tendency to overreact.

part five: About the Relationship
Keeping the Fire Going

Chapter 59 Let Go of His Half

1. Do you think that marriage is a 50/50 relationship?
2. Whom does the Lord consider that you ultimately serve in your role of wife (Colossians 3:23–25)?
3. What might be the result of choosing to practice your role as wife with excellence (1 Peter 3:1)?
4. How have you changed since you got married? Would your husband say that you have changed for the better or for the worse?
5. What does Jesus say a person should expect back from another person when she extends love (Luke 6:35)?

Chapter 60 and 61 Depart and Reunite/ Conduct a Hugging Class

Attentiveness to your husband as you depart for the day and reunite in the evening is one of the quickest ways to warm up your relationship.

1. How good are you at departures and reunions?
2. How do you send your husband off to work, or if you leave before he does, what is your departure like? Do you kiss him and tell him you love him?
3. How are your homecomings?

4. Are your departures and reunions mood-dependent (do they depend on your mood?)?
5. Would you be willing to try blastoff and reentry in your marriage for seven days *in a row?*

Chapter 62 Take Out the Garbage

1. How set in your ways are you?
2. How do issues like these become bigger than they really should be?
3. What can you do if this becomes a battle of wills (Colossians 3:12; James 4:6–8, 11)?
4. What would happen if you no longer mentioned the irritation and took care of the problem yourself? How do you think that would make you feel? Stronger or weaker? Why?

Chapter 63 Discern His Pet Peeves

1. What are your husband's pet peeves regarding conversation?
2. Do you nitpick at the way he speaks or tells stories?
3. How does this make a man feel?
4. How does this make a woman look?

Chapter 64 Avoid Arguments and Assumptions

1. What kind of damage might arguing do to a relationship?
2. What better ways can you better handle issues that come up (1 Corinthians 13:5)?

Chapter 65 Discover His Passions

1. If your husband asked, could you tell him what his passions are?
2. How do you help him realize his passions?
3. Since there is something that invigorates a man when he's dreaming out loud or living out his passions, what do you do that creates that kind of environment for him?

Chapter 66 Abolish the Cold Treatment

1. How often does your husband encounter cold treatment?
2. Does he generally know why, or is he clueless?
3. Why do you respond this way (Proverbs 29:11; Ephesians 4:26; James 1:19–20)?
4. Where did you learn it? How do you think you could unlearn it?

Chapter 67 Quit Keeping Score

1. What do you think delights the Lord (1 John 5:1–5)?
2. Why was the woman in Proverbs 31 able to laugh at the future (Proverbs 31:25)?
3. What happens when the Lord delights in you (Psalm 37:23)?
4. How can looking in the mirror of James 1:19–25 keep you from keeping score?

Chapter 68 Don't Go There!

1. How often do you visit "there" (Proverbs 15:1, 4)?
2. How do these verses help you avoid going "there"?

Chapter 69 The Skinny on Nagging

1. What do you do when you don't get what you want? What should you do (James 4:1–3)?
2. Do you think that you know more than your husband? If you do, and you make this obvious to him, how might he feel?
3. How should you interact with your husband (Philippians 2:14–16)?

Chapter 70 Don't Embarrass Your Husband

1. How can tendencies to embarrass your husband cause him to lose his trust in you (Proverbs 1:11–12)?

Chapter 71 When Your Warrior Is Tired

1. What does your warrior need when he is tired?
2. Have you thought to ask him?
3. How do you know when he is tired?
4. What you say to your husband when he is weary can have a profound impact on him. What have you been saying to him?
5. What changes might you need to make?

Chapter 72 Learn to Navigate Stormy Waters

1. How do men deal with storms differently than women do?
2. In the midst of a storm, how can you be a calming influence in his life?
3. How can *you* have perfect peace, even in the midst of the storm (Isaiah 26:3)?
4. The next time your husband faces a storm what will you do to say "I love you" or "I am with you"?
5. What has been your reaction to the storms in his life (Isaiah 41:10)?

Chapter 73 Making It to the Other Side

1. Do you expect your husband to act like you would in a given situation?
2. What do you do when he disappoints you?
3. What can you do when your husband fails to meet your needs (Luke 6:35; Isaiah 41:10; Hebrews 13:5–6)?

Chapter 74 Don't Make Him a "Project"

1. How have you made your husband a project?
2. What has been his response?
3. Why do you think women feel the need to change their husbands?
4. Whose responsibility is it to change them?

5. What does God often use to change a husband (1 Peter 3:1)?
6. What is the best thing a woman can do when she sees areas that need attention in her husband's life (James 5:13; Philippians 4:6)?

Chapter 75 Don't Expect Him to Meet All Your Needs

1. Who is the only One that can meet all your needs (Matthew 6:8; Philippians 4:9)?
2. Who best knows your needs?
3. What was your expectation concerning this topic when you got married?

Chapter 76 Laugh!

1. How frequently does your home ring out with laughter?
2. How carefully do you guard against sarcasm in your interactions?
3. How closely do you think joy is connected with laughter (Psalm 126)?

Chapter77 Humility? Are You Kidding?

1. What are some of the benefits of humility (Proverbs 11:2; 15:33; Matthew 18:4; 23:12; Luke 14:11; 18:14)?
2. What does God give to the humble? How are we to be "dressed" (Proverbs 3:34; 25:9; 1 Peter 5:5)?
3. What is the opposite of humility? How is this demonstrated in your marriage? If a lack of humility is a problem for you, what can you do about it?
4. List practical ways you can live out this verse (Philippians 2:3–4).
5. How can you be transformed from the inside out (2 Corinthians 3:18; Romans 12:1–2)?

Chapter 78 Consider Becoming a Servant

1. What is the first thought that comes to your mind when you think of being someone's servant? Is it a pleasant one (Matthew 20:28)?
2. Do you see serving another, especially your husband, as a high calling or a low one?
3. How has our culture wooed you into thinking that servanthood is for the lowly?
4. Whom are you serving when you serve others (Colossians 3:23)?
5. What is a result of serving (Colossians 3:24)?
6. What can you do when you feel like giving up (2 Chronicles 15:7–8; Hebrews 11:35)?
7. As you think of how you've lived your life thus far, what kind of reward might you receive? A great reward? A small reward? (*If you think it will be small, change!*)

We may have a tendency to remind ourselves that our husbands will one day have to answer to God for their lives. More important, we need to remember that one day *we* will answer to God for *our* choices. This is where we need to put our energy.... Not on worrying about our husband's choices. This will revolutionize your life and your marriage.

Printed in the United States
by Baker & Taylor Publisher Services